21/12/20

Finchley Church End

KT-195-507

I was in search of distant islands, in love with the idea that, on a patch of land, protected by a circumference of sea, the obligations and irritations of life would dissolve and a singular clarity of mind would descend.

Comparing the life of freedom of thirty years of extraordinary travel from the Faroe Islands to the Aegean, from the Galapagos to the Andaman Islands with a life of responsibility as a doctor, community member and parent approaching middle age, *Island Dreams* riffs on the twinned poles of rest and motion, independence and attachment, never more relevant than in today's perennially connected world.

Illustrated with maps throughout, this is a celebration of human adventures in the world and within our minds.

30131 05725281 6

LONDON BOROUGH OF BARNET

ISLAND DREAMS

ALSO BY GAVIN FRANCIS

True North: Travels in Arctic Europe
Empire Antarctica: Ice, Silence & Emperor Penguins
Adventures in Human Being
Shapeshifters: On Medicine & Human Change

ISLAND DREAMS

Mapping an Obsession

GAVIN FRANCIS

First published in Great Britain in 2020
by Canongate Books Ltd, 14 High Street, Edinburgh EH1 1TE

canongate.co.uk

1

Copyright © Gavin Francis, 2020

The right of Gavin Francis to be identified as the
author of this work has been asserted by him in accordance
with the Copyright, Designs and Patents Act 1988

Every effort has been made to trace copyright holders and
obtain their permission for the use of copyright material.
The publisher apologises for any errors or omissions and
would be grateful if notified of any corrections that should be
incorporated in future reprints or editions of this book.

British Library Cataloguing-in-Publication Data
A catalogue record for this book is available on
request from the British Library

ISBN 978 1 78689 818 0

Typeset in Baskerville by Biblichor Ltd, Edinburgh

Printed and bound in China by C&C Offset Printing Co., Ltd

CONTENTS

For my children.
I couldn't have hoped for finer
anchors, sails, ballast.

ORIGINS *of an* OBSESSION

HITCH-HIKING NORTH THROUGH the islands of Shetland a Land Rover stopped for me. The driver was a man of about forty; he wore a gas-blue boiler suit and his beard was flecked with white. *Where are you bound?* he asked, with a voice like rust and sea-spray, an accent more Norse than Scots.

Unst, I said.

He told me that off the island of Unst, the northernmost of the Shetland Islands, a black-browed albatross had been seen – a species accustomed to the skerries of the sub-Antarctic. *It must have crossed the equator in a storm*, he said, *and got disorientated. Took one look at Unst and thought, 'That looks like home.'*

I was in search of distant islands, in love with the idea that, on a patch of land, protected by a circumference of sea, the obligations and irritations of life would dissolve and a singular clarity of mind would descend. It proved more complicated than that.

Thinking of islands often returns me in memory to the municipal library I visited as a child. The library was one of

Skaw

Chiberstack

Lamba Ness

Burg Firth

Woodwick

Norwick

Huna

UNST

Harlswick

Vosgarth

Balta

Wyck

Scarbrugh Ness

Inara Voe

BALTA SOUND

Usound or Wya Bay

Mounes Ness

3

4

8 & 9

Li nga Weya

Half Grunie

Wederholm

Grunie

Linga

the grandest buildings in town – entered directly from the street through heavy brass doors, each one tessellated in panes of glass thick as lenses. By age eight or nine I'd exhausted the children's library and been given an adult borrower's ticket. But as my mother browsed the shelves, often as not I'd sit down on the scratchy carpet tiles and open an immense atlas, running my fingers over distant and unreachable archipelagos as if reading Braille. I hardly dared hope I'd reach any of them; that I have reached a few is something of a relief. And so the love of islands has always, for me, been inextricable from the love of maps.

Cartographers know that to isolate and distil the features of a portion of the earth's surface, in all its inexpressible complexity, is to exert power over it. To transfer that distillation onto paper is in some way to *encompass* it. But it could be said that maps offer only the illusion of understanding a landscape.

Encompass, from Latin *en*, meaning to make or put in, and *compass*, to surround, contain, envelop, enclose with steps (*com-passare*). Perhaps island maps, reined in by their coasts, offer a special case. They invite the viewer to indulge the imagination, pace a dreamed perimeter.

I've always found old maps intoxicating. In their wavering outlines, archaic scripts and obsolete navigational marks, they are palimpsests of the ways islands have been imagined over the centuries. In the famous world map in his atlas of 1570 Ortelius injected vast tracts of pure imagination, including a *river of islands* draining a mysterious southern continent.

By their omissions, all maps leave room

for the imagination, and for dreams.

However beautiful, with their ships and dragons, those old maps were tools of empire and capital. Science is how capitalism knows the world, a friend remarks to me, and the distinctions and details these maps marked out were first of all for merchants and military expeditions. What was marked 'Terra Incognita' was also what remained unvanquished.

REBECCA SOLNIT

The twelfth-century Chinese scholar Zheng Qiao wrote of the benefits of mingling textual and pictorial descriptions of landscape: *Images* (tu) *are the warp threads and the written words* (shu) *are the weft . . . To see the writing without the image is like hearing the voice without seeing the form; to see the image without the writing is like seeing a person but not hearing his words.*

Lewis

A few months after my voyage to Shetland, while hitch-hiking across the Hebridean island of Lewis, I met a French woman, nineteen years old, who'd received a government grant to travel around Scotland looking for fairies. She had pale blond hair like wisps of cirrostratus; archipelagos of freckles were dotted across her cheeks and nose. She told me she had little money left and often slept rough, painting pictures in exchange for meals – for paint she snapped open biro pens and mingled their contents with coffee.

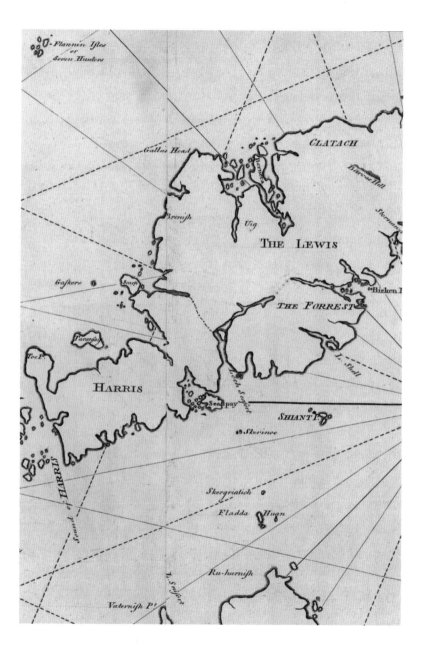

The same day I met a buzz-cut banker from New York who had quit his job to spend three months cycling around the Hebrides, hauling his surfboard behind him on a trailer. He had already cancelled his flight back. *I'd begun to doubt it was possible to feel this free,* he said.

Encounters in Unst and in Lewis reinforced to me that my fascination with islands – my *isle-o-philia* – was far from unique. There seemed to be a connection between a certain kind of sparsely populated island, remote from urban centres, and dreams. Or perhaps it is that such islands have the power of concentrating dreamers.

The word *isolate* comes from the adoption into English of the Italian *isolare*: to make into an island. About two centuries ago a critic wrote disparagingly of this new tendency to coin words from mainland Europe rather than stick with English Latinate equivalents, such as *insulate*. *We have here* evasion *for escape*, one wrote, *we have the unnecessary and foolish word* isolate.

I read Judith Schalansky's description of circling a man-high globe in Berlin, *reading the names of every tiny piece of land marooned in the breadth of the oceans . . . as full of promise as those white patches beyond the lines indicating the horizon of the known world drawn on old maps,* and thought of my own atlas-wanderings during the same years, cross-legged on the floor of a Scottish public library. On the blurb of Thurston Clarke's *Islomania* I read that islands *inspire feelings of great passion, serenity, and sometimes fear . . . they give people the opportunity to find themselves – or to lose their minds.*

At the time of making the journey to Shetland, and then to the Hebrides, my primary work was as a busy, metropolitan hospital doctor – an occupation noted for its frenetic demands, sleepless nights and hectic schedules of duty. I was in my mid-twenties; the life around and before me promised deepening connections to career, society, friends. *Why isolate yourself?* I'd think when, on being awarded a few days off, I stood again on a ferry, looking towards a blue horizon.

Between the attractions of isolation and of connection there was a tension that I didn't particularly attempt, or hope, to resolve.

What are my hopes for readers of these observations on islands? That they may read of an island in words, and then again on a map – in contours, harbours, beaches and rivers? That they may take a journey through a few islands of my acquaintance, and invest those same islands with dreams of their own?

And what do I hope to accomplish for myself – the resolution of the tension between isolation and connection? An assessment of the value of isolation in an increasingly connected world? Mapping them has been like conducting a chess match against myself – each move a nudge towards mutual triumph, stalemate, or mutual defeat.

Unst turned out to be a practical, working island, with a subdued tourist economy. The islanders' self-reliance was evident in the close correspondence between the surnames in the graveyard and those in the current phone directory: Petersson, Cluness, Ritch, Jamieson.

Muckle Flugga

Off the northern tip of the island, beyond the bird reserve of Herma Ness, were the islets of Muckle Flugga, the most northerly of the British Isles. Muckle Flugga, just a couple of hundred metres across, is famous for cliffs of breeding gannets where the albatross had felt so at home. *Muckle* means big in Old Norse, and *Flugga* connotes birds. Beyond it there was only Out Stack, a stubby pestle of stone ground smooth by the perpetual Atlantic swell.

Could it be that the love of islands is less a preference than a diagnosis? In his essay 'Communicating and Not Communicating', the psychoanalyst and paediatrician Donald Winnicott wrote: *The boy and girl at puberty can be described in many ways, and one way concerns the adolescent as an* isolate. *This preservation of personal isolation is part of the search for identity.* Winnicott goes on to propose that teenagers self-isolate from their parents and from their therapists because that's the only way they can find the space to summon an authentic self from the disorder of their experience. The trick to easing their distress, Winnicott suggested, was to create a therapeutic sense of isolation without allowing the adolescent to become *insulated* to the world. I am still figuring out what he meant by the distinction.

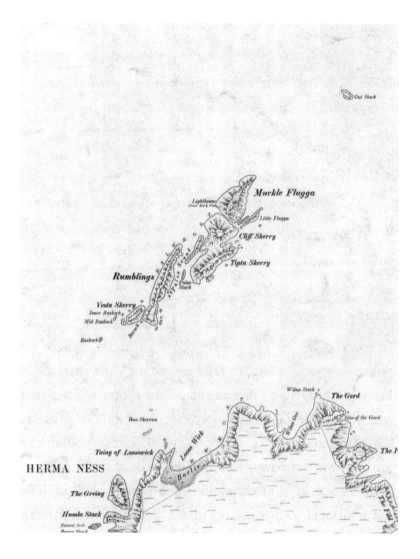

Out Stack

Muckle Flugga

Lighthouse
(Fixed, Red & White)

Little Flugga

Cliff Skerry

Tipta Skerry

Rumblings

Vesta Skerry

Inner Ruskock
Mid Ruskock

Ruskock

Wilna Stack

The Gord

Boa Skerries

Geo of the Gord

Wilna Geo

Tuing of Loosswick

Louns Wick

The F

HERMA NESS

Boelie

The Greing

Humla Stack

The Fill

Natural Arch
Burra Stack

I asked a psychoanalyst. *Isolation, for the adolescent, is a motor to leave the family,* he said. *If a child is raised in a way that is too idealising of childhood, then he or she has reduced motivation to undertake the tasks of adolescence – to develop a sense of the body, of sex, of work, of skills and aptitudes, of disidentifying from parents.*

This process can go too far, he added, and he began to speak to me of pathologies of the mind, of *autistic* and *psychotic* islands.

Now that smartphones can connect practically everyone, everywhere, it may be that the quality of isolation too has changed. To experience a hint of the thrill and the relief of being marooned, it's enough to simply *disconnect*.

Isle of May Through my own childhood and adolescence, family holidays were often to campsites on the Fife coast, where the estuary of the River Forth relaxes into the expansiveness of the North Sea. The Lothian side of the shore, where I now live, was visible on clear days along the southern horizon. This Fife coast was once home to Alexander Selkirk, a tanner's son born in 1676, who became a navigator and privateer – a kind of state-sponsored pirate – and in 1704 was marooned on an island in the South Pacific. Rescue came after four years and four months. His story inspired Daniel Defoe to write the tale of Robinson Crusoe.

My brother and I slept on camp beds in a caravan's curtainless awning – as I waited for sleep I'd count the firefly

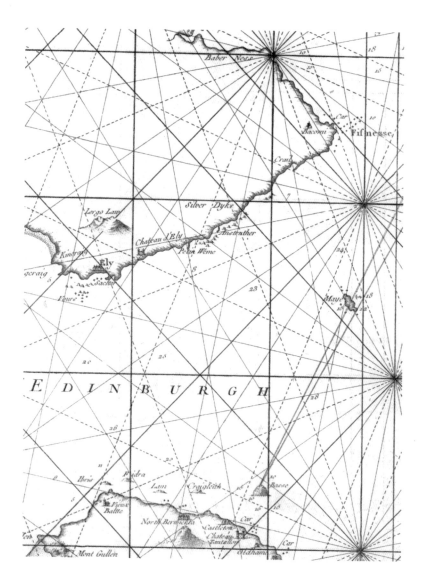

scintillation of lighthouses on the shorelines opposite. The nearest was the light on the Isle of May, part-way across the firth, which issued two white flashes every fifteen seconds.

One of the earliest lighthouses in northern Europe still stands on the May. It was a simple coal brazier atop a stone-built tower, first kindled in 1636. Selkirk would have sailed past it on his way to the high seas, and on his eventual return. I hoped one day to reach it.

As a boy I had a bowdlerised edition of *The Swiss Family Robinson*. The tale, written originally in German, is of a family shipwrecked on their way to Australia, forced to make an island life together, adopting *Robinson Crusoe* as a guide. The author was heavily influenced by the educational ideas of Rousseau. At the close of the family's decade of isolation some members opted for a return to civilisation, while others stayed on in what, to my mind, seemed a paradise. As it still does.

Shiant Isles

At age twenty-one the writer Adam Nicolson inherited the Shiant Isles, a tiny archipelago between the Scottish mainland and the Hebridean island of Lewis. In his book about them, *Sea Room*, he wrote: *Perhaps . . . the love of islands is a symptom of immaturity, a turning away from the complexities of the real world to a much simpler place, where choices are obvious and rewards straightforward. And perhaps that can be taken another step: is the whole Romantic episode,*

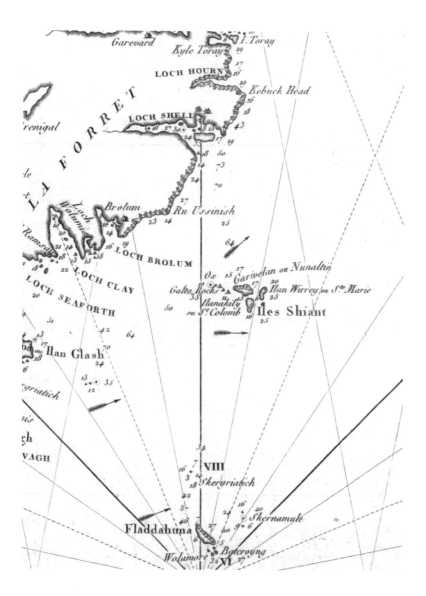

Garevard *I. Toray*

Kyle Toray

LOCH HOURN

Kebuck Head

LOCH SHELL

renigal

L A   F O R R E T

Brolum   *Ru Ussinish*

LOCH BROLUM

Gariveilan ou Nunaltin

LOCH CLAY   Ox

Galta Rocks   Ilan Wirrey ou Ste Marie

LOCH SEAFORTH   Ilanakily   **Iles Shiant**
ou St Colomb

Ilan Glash

VIII
Skergriatich

Fladdahuna   Skernamule

Wolamore   Botcroyng
XI

from Rousseau to Lawrence, a vastly enlarged and egotist- ical adolescence?

My work as a physician requires immersion in the complexities of human relationships. Few jobs are better suited to someone interested in what motivates and inspires human beings, and what connects them.

But through adolescence, medical school, and working as a doctor in speciality training, it began to dawn on me that I sought out islands to recalibrate my sense of what matters. Their absence of connection, their *isolation*, was therapeutic in a way I found difficult to articulate.

Treasure Island

When I first saw Muckle Flugga, like the albatross I too thought it looked like home. A lighthouse built in the nineteenth century by the famous Stevenson family clings limpet-like to its highest ridge. It is lapped on the west by the Atlantic, and on the east by the North Sea. During its construction it was visited by a son of the family, the young Robert Louis Stevenson (the lighthouse was completed in 1858), and a legend exists that his map of Treasure Island is based on the outline of Unst.

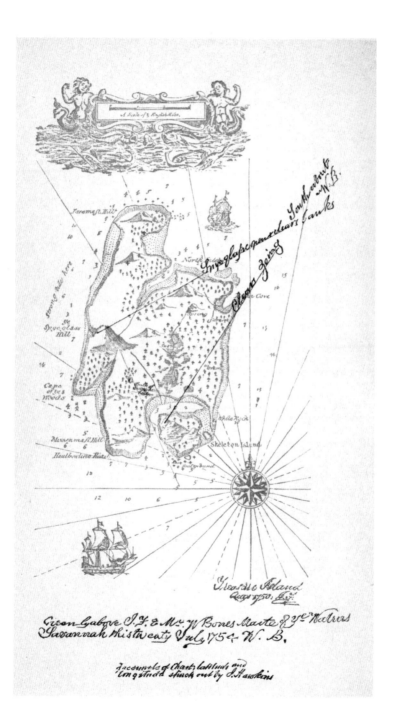

A Scale of 3 English Miles.

Tarem st. Hill

North inlet

Spye glass Hill

Cape of the Woods

Skeleton Island

Treasure Island

Aug st 1750. W.B.

Given above J.F. & Mr W. Bones Maste of ye Walrus
Savannah this Twenty July 1754. W.B.

Facsimile of Chart latitude and
Longitude struck out by J. Hawkins

In my home town of Edinburgh I often pass the head-quarters of the Northern Lighthouse Board, announced at eye level on a neat Georgian street by a polished brass plaque. The board's insignia is a white minaret of a light-house on a background of Iznik blue, towering over a shallow bowl of white-topped Hokusai waves. The waves are saw-like, breaking over a serration of black rocks so neatly that it's difficult, at first, to tell where the waves end and where the foundations of the lighthouse begin. Like Virginia Woolf's, it is *a stark tower on a bare rock*.

In Salutem Omnium – 'for the safety of all' – is written in letters of gold on a banner draped around the tower's lantern house.

Like a pilot who sleeps best by a runway, I sleep easiest within sight of the sea.

REVERENCE,
TRANSFORMATION

THAT FIRST TIME in Unst I camped on the northernmost bluff, surrounded by the burrows of puffins, my
tent strobed through the short night by beams from Stevenson's lighthouse. Cormorants on the rocks below lined up
as if listening to the weather's sermon. Puffins returning to
their burrows fussed around my ankles. The horizon was
shaded in subtle laminations as it stretched towards the
Arctic Ocean, blue to deepest scarlet, and the cliffs were in
bloom with little white trumpets of sea campion and purple
rosettes of thrift. There were no other flowers: these two
species seemed uniquely adapted to the asperities of the
North Atlantic fringe.

Around 1,500 years ago an Irish monk known as Brendan
explored the archipelagos north and west of the island of
Britain – his oral account has survived in a Latin text dated
to the ninth century, the *Navigatio Sancti Brendani Abbatis*.
The *Navigatio* sees Brendan and his companions beaching
their leather boat on an island carpeted in flowers of white
and purple. White, the narrator informs us, represents inno-
cence. Purple, on the other hand, with its undertones of
papal, imperial and Byzantine authority, represents maturity.

Brendan's island is host to a monastic community and its members dress in white or purple according to their age. Brendan names it *the island of steadfast men*. One of his companions decides to abandon their voyage and, with Brendan's blessing, joins the monks.

Islands may be sought out as testing grounds for youth, as catalysts of transformation, as midwives to maturity. Helen Dunmore, in her essay on Woolf's *To the Lighthouse*, writes: *James, at six years old, hates his father as much as he loves his mother. Only a gash from a poker or a thrust from a knife into Mr Ramsay's heart will ease James's furious humiliation. James sustains his hatred for a decade, and, when the voyage to the lighthouse does at last take place, it seems that he will get his chance to lock antlers with his father.*

Woolf's fictional lighthouse was off the Isle of Skye, but was inspired by the light on Godrevy Island, just off the north coast of Cornwall, and within sight of the holiday house she frequented as a child. It's in Cornwall that she may first have read Defoe's *Robinson Crusoe*, of which she wrote: *To dig, to bake, to plant, to build – how serious these simple occupations are. Hatchets, scissors, logs, axes – how beautiful these simple objects are.*

Is this the value of islands, that they *simplify*?

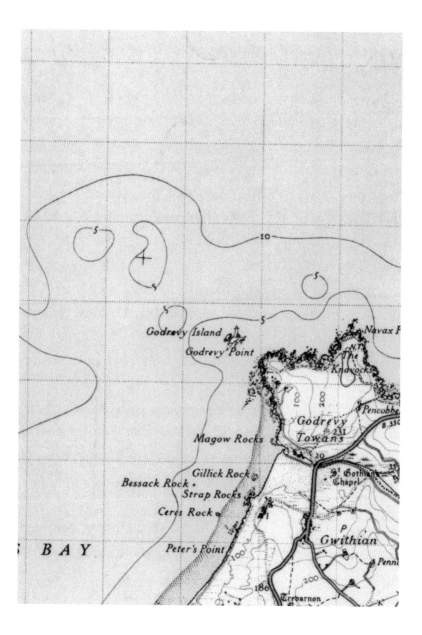

In *Letters from Iceland* Louis MacNeice wrote of his gaiety at having come north, running away from what he saw as the south's 'cruel clocks' and surfeit of books, cushions and yelling newsboys. In the monastic isolation of Iceland he hoped to achieve a measure of freedom from *the ambushes of sex* and the drive to retrieve *significance from the river of passing people.*

Retrieving significance from rivers of passing people is a fair summary of the satisfactions of medical practice. William Carlos Williams wrote of his pleasure in being intimately connected to the lives of others through doctoring. *Was I not interested in man?* he wrote. *There the thing was, right in front of me.*

André Malraux, the French novelist, adventurer and Resistance fighter, relates in his *Anti-Memoirs* what a priest felt a lifetime of hearing confessions has taught him (an assessment that could just as easily have been uttered by a physician as a priest).

'*First of all, that people are much more unhappy than one thinks . . . and then . . .*' *He raised his brawny lumberman's arms in the starlit night;* '*And then, the fundamental fact is that* there is no such thing as a grown-up person.'

A mentor I once worked for, in the Highlands of Scotland, said to me: *You don't need to be a special kind of doctor to work on an island, you just need to be a very good one.*

Winnicott believed that in order to pass through the testing grounds of adolescence, to scorch away those elements of our childhood selves that we must necessarily discard, but anneal other elements into the stability of our adult identities, it was important to cultivate a sense of isolation. But in a world where every adolescent has a smartphone it's not clear what Winnicott's sense of isolation could mean.

I seldom work in hospitals now; the majority of my medical work takes place in a small community clinic near Edinburgh's city centre. Over the past decade, as online connectivity has increased, so has the frequency with which I see adolescents suffering clinical levels of anxiety. More and more, evidence on social media use suggests that too much connection to the lives of others carries risk.

W.B. Yeats's happiest childhood memories were of summers spent on a small lake-island in County Sligo. As a young man, walking the streets of London, his fantasy of return inspired one of his most treasured poems, 'The Lake Isle of Innisfree'.

I will arise and go now, and go to Innisfree, he wrote. *And I shall have some peace there, for peace comes dropping slow.*

I had still the ambition, formed in Sligo in my teens, of living in imitation of Thoreau on Innisfree. And when walking through Fleet Street, very homesick, I heard a little tinkle of water and saw a fountain in a shop window which balanced a little ball upon its jet, and began to remember lake water.

W.B. YEATS

The Christmas I was ten I was given a book of paintings and sketches from the Isle of May: *One Man's Island* by Keith Brockie. It began with an aerial photograph of the May, the Fife coast just visible in the frame's upper margin, and beside that the artist's impression of the same photograph with all the names of the landscape carefully pencilled in. I read and reread the names: North Ness and Altarstanes, Tarbet Hole and Maiden Hair.

The book was arranged thematically in four sections: Breeding Birds, Other Wildlife, Migrant Birds, and Grey Seals. It was the migrant section I turned to most often, leafing through intricately executed drawings of birds I'd never seen that Brockie had pulled from the mist nets and Heligoland traps on the island. Phalarope, bluethroat, redstart, wryneck, fieldfare, whimbrel, goldcrest: their names were an incantation, seductive exoticism inseparable from their island provenance. Brockie found a pair of goldcrests dead, and sketched them side by side. *Unfortunately many succumb to exhaustion, to the rain and cold wind*, he wrote beside the birds in tiny, spidered lettering.

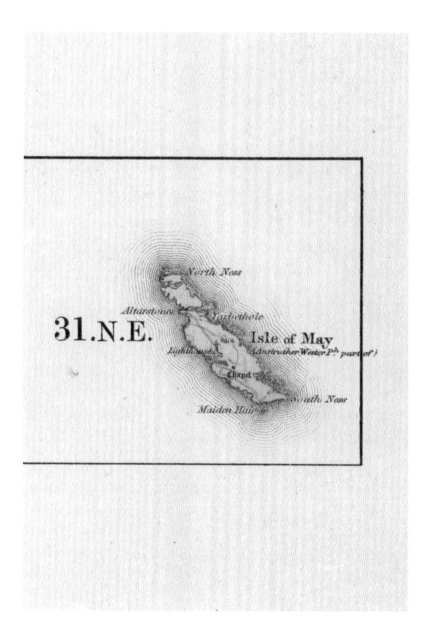

In Lerwick, Shetland, on my return from Unst, I drank in a pub named for *Ultima Thule* – the island imagined by the Greeks as a kind of punctuation mark at the end of the world – and in the local museum picked through memorabilia gathered the length of the axis of the Atlantic, Arctic to Antarctic, by Shetland whalemen. A map of their sea routes was a cat's cradle of connections.

Connection: the word dates in English from the fifteenth century, when European mariners began forging links between continents that had hitherto been isolated. *Con* meaning together, and *nectere* meaning to bind or tie.

The American mariner Joshua Slocum traversed the Atlantic three times on his famous circumnavigation of the globe between 1895 and 1898. Of the Azores he wrote: *Islanders are always the kindest people in the world, and I met none anywhere kinder than the good hearts of this place . . . The burden of taxes is heavy, with scant privileges in return, the air they breathe being about the only thing that is not taxed.*

His message? *There are costs to island living.*

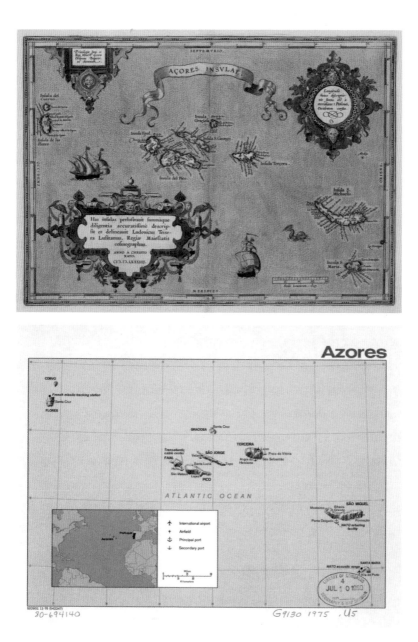

80-694140

G9130 1975 .U5

Samoa

Robert Louis Stevenson's love of islands may have been kindled in Shetland. He died on the island of Upolu, part of Samoa, a long way from his home town of Edinburgh, which he had grown to dislike. He was just forty-four.

By removing himself to Samoa, away from the demanding literary scenes of London and New York, Stevenson satisfied his hunger for a retreat into simplicity. Yeats had dreamed of planting bean rows on Innisfree; on Upolu Stevenson spent much of his time gardening. *I know pleasure still; pleasure with a thousand faces, and none perfect* he wrote to his friend, the literary critic Sidney Colvin. *High among these I place this delight of weeding out here alone by the garrulous water, under the silence of the high wood, broken by the incongruous sounds of birds. And take my life all through, look at it fore and back, and upside down, – though I would very fain change myself, I would not change my circumstances.*

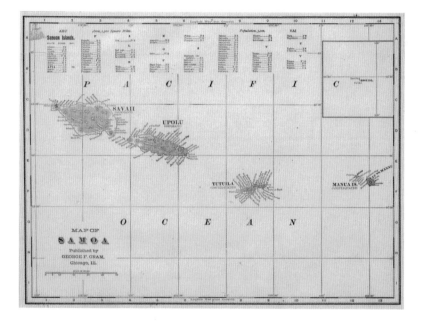

MAP OF
SAMOA
Published by
GEORGE F. CRAM,
Chicago, Ill.

Slocum, a man who knew a great deal about the benefits of isolation, arrived in Samoa not long after Stevenson's death from a brain haemorrhage, and was shown around the island by his widow.

A feeling of awe crept over me. My memory worked with startling power. The ominous, the insignificant, the great, the small, the wonderful, the commonplace – all appeared before my mental vision in magical succession. Pages of my history were recalled which had been so long forgotten that they seemed to belong to a previous existence. I heard all the voices of the past laughing, crying, telling what I had heard them tell in many corners of the earth.

JOSHUA SLOCUM

In Sara Maitland's *A Book of Silence* there's a passage where she describes the noises of remote isolation, the sounds of silence: *very low volume, continuous, and (usually) two or more toned.* She wonders whether those two tones are related to the function of the nervous system (high tone) and the blood (lower tone), as John Cage proposed in dialogues around his silent performance piece *4'33"*, or whether they're related to something more prosaic: particle movement in the inner ear, the noise of an overpopulated planet, the spinning of the universe, the slow creep of tectonic plates.

She wonders if the sound could represent the voice of God.

Or perhaps they're related to the *sounds and sweet airs* Caliban hears on his island, as he drifts between wakefulness and dreaming: *Be not afeard. The isle is full of noises.*

That sense of awe or reverence, of seeking after the sublime, that so many others have sought and found in islands, has without doubt influenced my love of them. This may have been what first drew me to Iona, an island off the west coast of Scotland, and the adopted home of Brendan's contemporary Columba. Columba sailed there from Ireland on the same kind of leather boat Brendan used. In common with many of the islands I've been writing about, Iona is often now considered 'remote'; but when people connected more easily by sea than by land, it was much less so. For Columba, Iona was central to the Irish world. This was a time of shifting borders: Irish *Scoti* pushing east into the lands of the Picts.

Iona

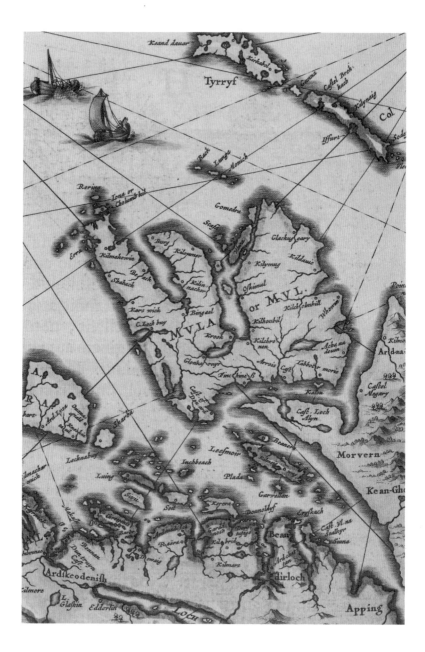

Ksand dauar

Tyrryf

Kirkabol

Genna

Caftel Brch. kach

Kelynaig

Col.

Iffurt

Sode

Back

Lunga

Monich

Rering

Iona or
Cholumb kil

Gomedra

Glacku gary

Errie

Kilmakewin

Bu ack

Burg

Scaf

Kilomer

Killauic

Shaback

Kilin
nachos

Kilymug

Oskimul

Killauic

Kilcholmkill

Whovin

Kars wich

Bingael

MVIA

Krook

or MVL.

Kilchro
nen

Ard-na-

C. Loch buy

Kilhoubill

Ara.

Ard Lyfa

Glonhas enga

Finc hine fs

Arois

Kilchre
nen

Acha na
deuin

Labbotar morie

Kihn

Donnae
quail

Caft. af

Ratton

Cagl

Caftel
Megary

Skarba

Caft. Loch
Alyn

Lecknabug

Leefmoir

Beanen

Morvern

Inchbeach

Plada

Luing

Ke an-Gh

Sieil

Seil

Kerera

Garvellan

Carigion

Dounolyf

Eryfkach

Beam

Caft. vl. na
Stalkyr

Barra

Andlackloch

mach

lufage

Kilbrid

Sinna

Roaira

Dowais

Kilmare

Ardchatan

Ardikeodenish

Dun Trym
Caftl

 Filirloch

Apping

Kilmore

L.
Glashin

Edderlin

LOCH

I arrived in Iona with a friend on Easter Saturday, and pitched camp out on the western shore. Next day we watched a young man, wearing a crown of thorns, drag a cross across the thrift towards the restored medieval abbey, followed by a crowd singing in harmony *Lord have mercy on us*. A woman sat weeping in the churchyard corner beneath placards plastered with newspaper headlines screaming of war and death. A shout went out for volunteers to take a turn carrying the cross, but I didn't step forward. I had the feeling that my redemption, such as it might be, lay elsewhere.

John Berger once travelled this western seaboard of Scotland. On the small island of Gigha, between the Kintyre peninsula and Islay, he walked amongst the graves of a coastal cemetery and his mind turned not to death, but to new life. *The sparsely inhabited coast of the continent here is shaped like the passage for a birth outward,* he wrote, *a uterus leading toward the western horizon.*

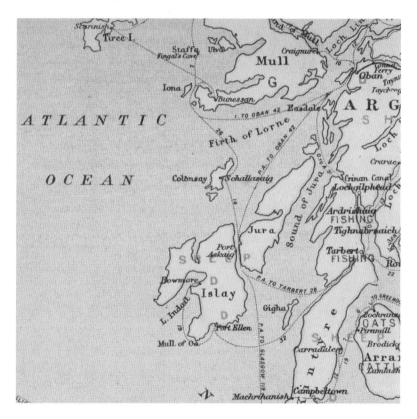

In the ancient Canaanite language known as Ugaritic the word for sea indicated the presence of a deity. The ocean, and the worship of the ocean, were indivisible.

Some years ago, following a spell working at a hospital in Kenya, I took a fly-blown, exhausting trip up the coast of east Africa. Tourism had plummeted following riots in Nairobi and Mombasa. Desperation had proven fertile ground for corruption. The journey was harrowing, until I took a boat from the African shore out to the island of Lamu.

The last few steps of my journey were by moonlight, wading with trousers rolled up, rucksack balanced on my head. The people of Lamu moved with a gentler flow, it seemed to me then, than they did on the continent I'd just left.

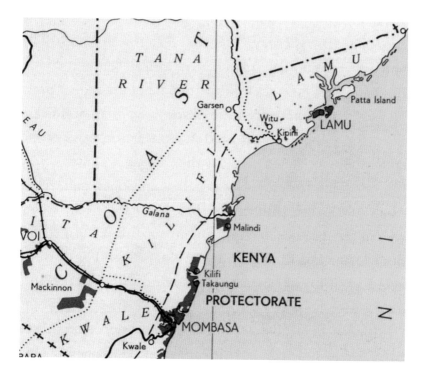

The streets were narrow and dark, but welcoming, and alive with the laughter of children. There were well-lit shops and cafés; men in long white robes lounged together, chatting. Rich fabrics hung over doorways. Women sat in huddles, turning to smile as I walked past. The air was heavy with perfumes. *This place is safe*, I thought. *No harm will come to me here.*

For Europe is absent.
This is an island and therefore
Unreal.

W.H. AUDEN

There are costs to island living, said Joshua Slocum. *The burden of taxes is heavy, with scant privilege in return.* The only other island I visited on that African journey was in the midst of a lake, itself in the middle of a national park. I'd paid an entrance fee to the park, bought an admission ticket for a country club hotel (it owned a tranche of the lake's shoreline), then paid another fee for a charter boat. On the island giraffes, wildebeest, antelopes and zebra ranged freely and without fear. Blue walls of the Rift Valley rose in the distance, merging into the azure sky. An equatorial light gave brilliance to the landscape. The warden asked me if I could sponsor him to find work in Europe. *I hate it here*, he said.

Islands may liberate, but also imprison. They *captivate*. I remembered the African warden's claustrophobia when, some years later, I took a post as a nature warden on the Scottish isle I'd watched and imagined on my childhood camping trips – the Isle of May.

The difference being that my post, of course, was temporary, and the arrangement voluntary. A condition of tolerating island life might well be the capacity to escape it.

The view of Henry David Thoreau was that we are forever isolated from one another – an archipelago of individuals. He professed little interest in travel, and singled out the remote Sandwich Islands (the name Cook gave to Hawaii), as a place he'd have no interest in hearing about. His preference, he said, was to hear about New England, from New Englanders. *I, on my side, require of every writer, first or last, a simple and sincere account of his own life, and not merely what he has heard of other men's lives; some such account as he would send to his kindred from a distant land; for if he has lived sincerely, it must have been in a distant land to me.*

Hawaii

I disagree with Thoreau: the ways of the Hawaiians are of great interest. Here is Charles Darwin, in *The Expression of Emotion in Man and Animals*, on their qualities: *With the Sandwich Islanders . . . tears are actually recognized as a sign of happiness.*

Darwin realised that Galapagos finches achieved their glorious, notorious diversity thanks to their literal and littoral isolation; with his story from Hawaii, he suggests the same is true of human beings.

Thoreau sought to make a peace between the pull he felt towards the woods, and the pull he felt to engage in the intellectual, social and physical pleasures of society. That seems a fair summary of what I'm attempting here: a simple and sincere cartography of my own obsession with the twinned but opposing allures of island and city, of isolation and connection.

I keep a bottle of Walden water at home on the windowsill; sunlight refracts through it. *It was a lake of rainbow light, in which, for a short while, I lived like a dolphin*, wrote Thoreau. *If it had lasted longer it might have tinged my employments and life.*

He knew that his life at Walden Pond could only ever be a temporary arrangement.

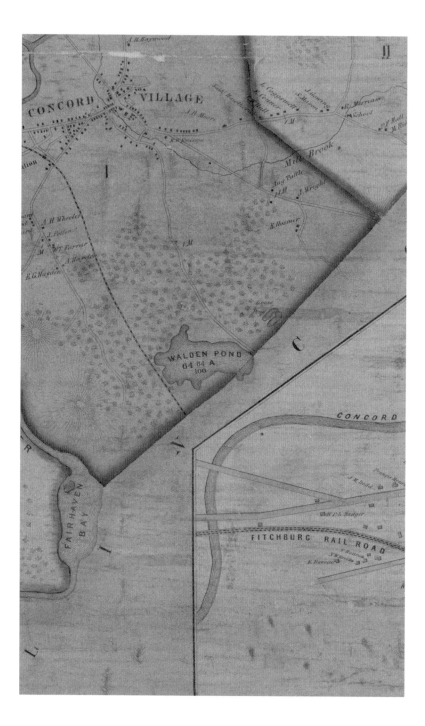

Thoreau's lake is an island in negative:

The landscape's most beautiful and expressive feature. It is the earth's eye, looking into which the beholder measures the depth of his own nature.

The pure Walden water is mingled with the sacred water of the Ganges, he also wrote, fresh from reading the *Bhagavad Gita. With favoring winds it is wafted past the site of the fabulous islands of Atlantis and the Hesperides, makes the periplus of Hanno, and, floating by Ternate and Tidore and the mouth of the Persian Gulf, melts in the tropic gales of the Indian seas.*

His view recalls the geography of the *Odyssey*, which imagines the vastness of the ocean as all-enveloping, all-encompassing mother. For Homer, the shield of the earth floated in the waters of the ocean the way an embryo floats in amniotic fluid. It isolates, as Winnicott said a good parent should, without *insulating*.

There are scholars who suspect that each island encountered in the *Odyssey* represents a stage in a mnemonic technique, that Homer paces Odysseus's path across an island framework of memory. But at the same time each is a world unto itself, a pure challenge to overcome, leading the listener on. The *Odyssey* makes it obvious that islands can be testing grounds, way stations in the storm of life.

In writing these observations on islands, I'm aware of casting my mind back across thirty years of journeys, the islands serving as stepping stones into memory, each one illustrative of a turn taken in life – a phase of reflection or change.

In Kenya I'd often been the palest and hottest person on any given street. I began to yearn for a place I'd be inconspicuous and cool. After just a few days home in Edinburgh I caught a boat to Bergen in Norway. From Bergen I went by train to Bodø, then took a ferry to the Arctic archipelago of Lofoten. There I fell in with a French couple of isle-o-philes: Claire and Jean-Baptiste. My French was poor (as it still is), so their company came with a measure of welcome isolation.

The slopes of the Lofoten mountains were carpeted in a thick moss that moulded itself around my body as I slept; the tensions of those African journeys dissolved. We climbed a mountain overlooking the original Maelstrom, a tidal whirlpool between two of the islands. My sleep was interrupted by the croaking of ravens. About midnight one night I was woken by Claire to see an aurora borealis. The lights were just beginning, a small flame of grey haze against the night. From the clifftop we watched them multiply, columns of green conjured from nothing, only to flourish and then evanesce. A wash of swirling luminescence rose and fell, like marbled endpapers spread over the book of the sea. Meteorites flashed through the ionosphere and, at one moment, standing high on the island ridge, I was surrounded on all sides by vertical pillars of grey-green light stretching up to infinity. Sometimes the flames came quickly, but more often they moved imperceptibly, so that as I turned my attention away from one part of the horizon and back, I hadn't noticed any movement but the scene had changed.

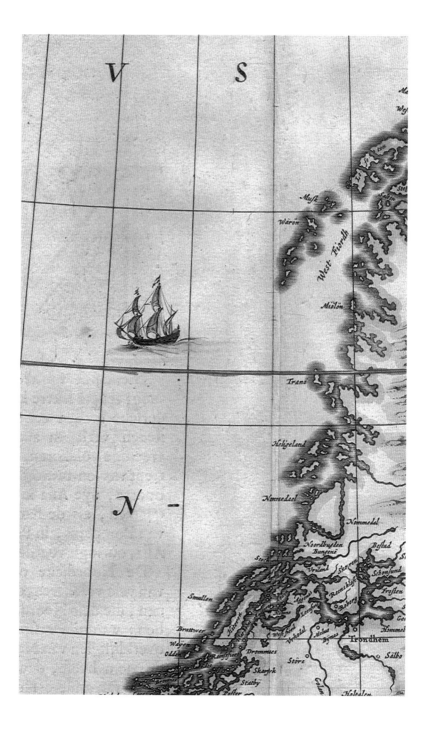

I sat up watching the lights until the filament of crimson along the northern horizon fattened to a dull dawn. More light rose from the horizon in chromatography columns, dissolving the aurora into the gathering day.

Edgar Allan Poe never visited the Lofoten Islands, but summoned them in the imagination: *A panorama more deplorably desolate no human imagination can conceive*, he wrote, inaccurately. *To the right and left, as far as the eye could reach, there lay outstretched, like ramparts of the world, lines of horridly black and beetling cliffs.*

My isolation in the Lofoten Islands was, I felt then, entirely beneficial – even therapeutic. Later, I asked another psychoanalyst about Winnicott's distinction between the psychological state of *isolation*, which was to be cherished, and *insulation*, which was to be abhorred.

This is one of Winnicott's more obscure essays, he said, *but a powerful one.* He went on to explain that, for Winnicott, we each carry a true self deep within us, but show a variety of changeable false selves depending on the demands of each particular moment.

False selves? I asked.

Like the fast-food waitress who says 'Enjoy your day!', he explained. *That's a false self. The insulated person is one who no longer has any lines of communication between the false self and the true self. They no longer know what's true. They're all alone.*

PEACE & IMPRISONMENT

I THINK OF that journey to the Lofoten Islands now, from a distance of more than twenty years, with a tender gratitude – that I should have been so fortunate as to have made their acquaintance at that time when I needed rest, silence and isolation. *I wander about the island as usual, thinking of this and that,* wrote the Norwegian writer Knut Hamsun. *Peace, peace, a heavenly peace speaks to me in muted tones from every tree in the forest.*

When Napoleon and Tsar Alexander wanted to make peace, on the banks of the River Nemen, no island was available. It was resolved that one should be constructed. A barge was moored at the midpoint of the river and towering white tents were erected, embroidered respectively 'N' and 'A'.

Sire, I hate the English no less than you do and I am ready to assist you in any enterprise against them, Alexander is supposed to have said as the two men met on the barge.

In that case everything can be speedily settled between us and peace made, replied Napoleon.

Of course Napoleon came to know islands less for their ability to promote peace, than to imprison – as he was imprisoned on Elba and on St Helena.

There are many other prison islands: Andaman, Alcatraz, Robben, Île Sainte-Marguerite, Rikers, Château d'If, the Bass Rock, Hashima. Even Ellis Island was chosen for its holding properties, its *containment*.

From Chennai in India I once took a plane to the Andaman Islands, midway across the Bay of Bengal. Under British rule the archipelago had been a penal colony, but from the air they looked more like paradise than penitentiary: islets of palm trees haloed by crayon-yellow sand, scattered across a sea as blue and translucent as Murano glass.

On the ground the heat was like a migraine, pounding and shimmering, fracturing the light. I queued for a landing permit behind an extended matriarchal family of Tamils, the long plaits of the women braided with jasmine blossom. Behind me there were ten or fifteen Israelis recently demobbed from war in South Lebanon. The fort was sun-bleached; we were invited to walk among the cells where up to 12,000 Indian political dissidents who had fought against British rule had been chained, whipped, forced to grind nuts for oil and pound coconuts for coir fibres. Prisoners were often summarily executed. The suicide rate was high. On a visit in 1872 the British viceroy, Lord Mayo, was stabbed to death by an inmate.

They used to hang people three at a time on the prison gallows. On the day I visited, they were sticky with fresh paint.

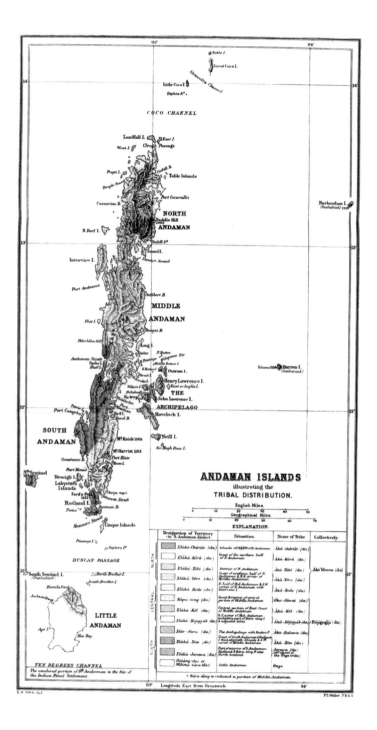

There are tribes living on some of the remoter islands of the archipelago who remain entirely without any contact with the modern, connected world. It's forbidden to put ashore on these islands. Recently an American missionary who tried to land on North Sentinel Island was killed by its islanders.

On the ferry to Neill Island, one of the islets of the Andamans, I noticed how different the air had felt sailing earlier that year on a Scottish ferry, but how startlingly familiar the ferry itself was – a great steel vessel of rust caked in layers of white gloss, garlanded with lifeboats, its flip-up seats stuffed with orange safety vests. The sea was a shade of iridescent turquoise – a thin pale bar of coastal sand plummeted to a deep, almost phosphorescent blue. Small salvos of flying fish whirred from the water like clockwork toys. Dolphins bounced ahead of the prow.

On the island a track led down to a beach where four huts were arranged in a horseshoe. The only other residents were an Israeli couple who'd been there a week. He was from a small kibbutz in the Negev, she from the Sea of Galilee. They spoke of their reluctance to fight, the abomination of war, of the erosion of their loyalty towards the commanders who gave the orders. The man told me that he'd never experienced freedom until now, on this tropical beach.

We lit a fire. They passed a home-made narghile pipe between themselves. The sand was very fine, studded with tiny cowries and pieces of broken coral. *I wish I didn't have to go back*, the woman said.

Well, don't, I said. Though I knew that I too would soon be obliged to return.

'We're the last ones here. I've no idea when we'll go, but my brother and sister are in Hebron.' She did not know that this was a Jewish island in an Arab sea.

COLIN THUBRON

Despite their proximity to Myanmar, the Andaman Islands run on Indian time. At 4.30 a.m. I stood waist-deep in the sea, watching the sunrise with two Brahmins from Delhi, thinking of a monk I met once who imagined he felt divine love waxing and waning on his skin. The sun rose quickly over a scarlet bank of cloud, a liniment over the wound of the horizon.

By 6 a.m. dawn was a beach in the sky, yellow and endless. I pedalled back to my hut and ate *thali* for breakfast, regretting the necessity of my departure.

Inch Garvie In Scotland I sleep a hundred yards from a firth dividing two lands that, many centuries ago, were considered different countries: Fife and Lothian. In 832 an island at its midpoint, an island I see every morning as I open my curtains, saw the forging of an uneasy peace. A defeated king of Lothian and Northumberland, King Athelstane, was decapitated by Angus, the Pictish king of the lands to the north. Athelstane's head was displayed on the island as a warning to any who would try to cross to Fife.

A bridge stanchion rests on it now, a friendlier emblem of reconciliation.

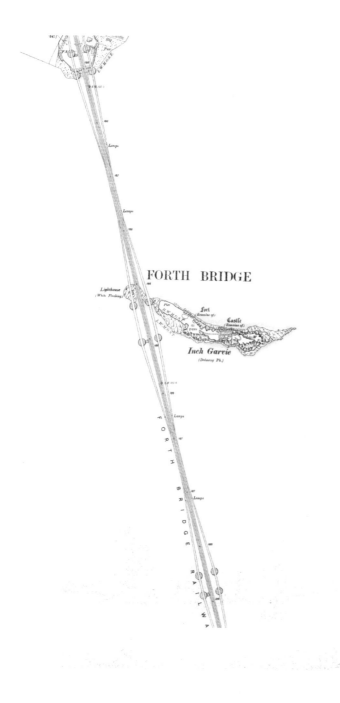

FORTH BRIDGE

Lighthouse
(White Flashing)

Fort
(Remains of)

Castle
(Remains of)

Inch Garvie
(Disusing Ph.)

FORTH BRIDGE RAILWAY

Further downstream is the holy island of Inchcolm, also known as the *Iona of the East*.

Further yet is the prison island of the Bass Rock, a volcanic plug rising sheer from the sea.

Gannets thrive on it, so many that the Linnaean identifier of the species is *bassanus* – 'of the Bass'. To the Spanish the gannet is known as *alcatraz*, an Arabic word meaning 'the diver'.

And in the same estuary is the island of Inchkeith, once *Inchkeith* Edinburgh's leprosarium, now the possession of an absentee landlord who made millions fitting car tyres.

A year after Columbus breached the microbial isolation of the Americas with the smallpox virus, a king in Edinburgh, James IV, conceived an experiment on Inchkeith to reveal the language of angels. A near contemporary, the historian Robert Lyndsay, wrote of the experiment (the following translated into modern English):

He ordered them to take a mute woman and to put her in Inchkeith, to give her two children, and to provide her with everything she would need for their nourishment. His goal was to discover what language the children would speak when they were old enough to have 'perfect' speech. Some say they spoke good Hebrew, but I do not know of any reliable sources for these claims.

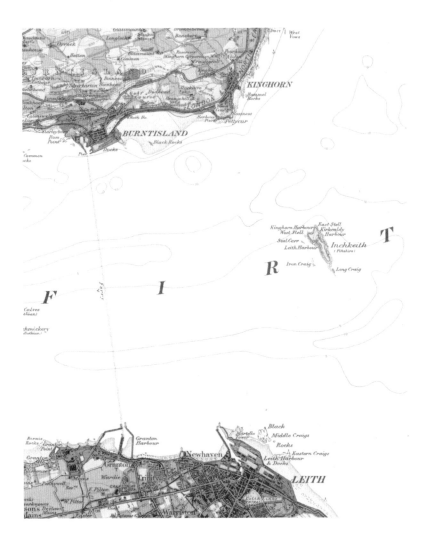

Beyond this, the historical record is silent. When I imagine the infant speech of those children, it's not the speech of angels that I imagine, but the cries of gulls, the spray of waves, the susurration of wind over rough stone.

A pitiless place: four years later the record suggests that the nurse and the two children were removed. In 1497 it was decided that Edinburgh sufferers of syphilis, plague and leprosy would be transported by ship to die on Inchkeith. For three hundred years it remained a place of pestilence and quarantine.

One November at the close of the millennium, when I was starting out as a junior surgical trainee, I left the hospital wards behind for a week's camping in the Hebridean island of Barra. The forecast was for storms: after a couple of nights in a shaking tent I swapped canvas for a hotel room, and set up my camp stove in the en-suite bath. Each day I walked: over the high blustery freedom of Ben Scurrival, around the western reaches of the island, down to Vatersay Sound, across beaches raked by waves. There were families of otters, endless horizons, abandoned homesteads, inquisitive seals. There was a beach that doubled as an airport runway, its landing timetable rotating with the tide.

The open bays were chopped into textual, symmetrical lines of waves. The agitation kindled by my hospital work was gradually extinguished. As the days passed I began muttering as I walked, random subconscious connections, snatches of songs, memories. Their content didn't seem to matter, my voice being lost in the sound of the wind and waves.

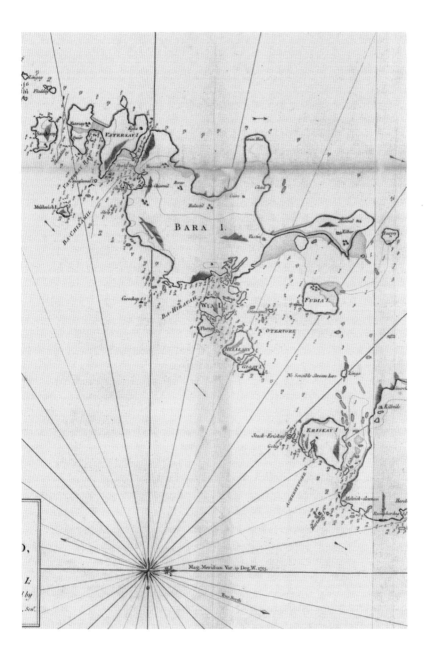

BOOKS *of* DISTANT
ISLANDS

LOUIS MACNEICE FLED to the islands in part to escape an *excess of books*. Perhaps he needed isolation from language in order to clear his mind. But that has never been true for me – of the islands I've cherished most, I met many first in print.

I first encountered the Pacific island of Chiloé, and its poverty, through the books of two English travellers, Charles Darwin and Bruce Chatwin: *The Voyage of the Beagle* and *In Patagonia*. Of the main town in Chiloé – Castro – Darwin wrote: *The poverty of the place may be conceived from the fact, that although containing some hundreds of inhabitants, one of our party was unable anywhere to purchase either a pound of sugar or an ordinary knife.*

In the same town, more than a century and a half later, I was unable to purchase so much as a cheap watch. Darwin: *No individual possessed either a watch or a clock: and an old man, who was supposed to have a good idea of the time, was employed to strike the church bell by guess.* Perhaps the passing of time has less traction on the minds of Chiloé's inhabitants than it does on the mainland.

Chiloé

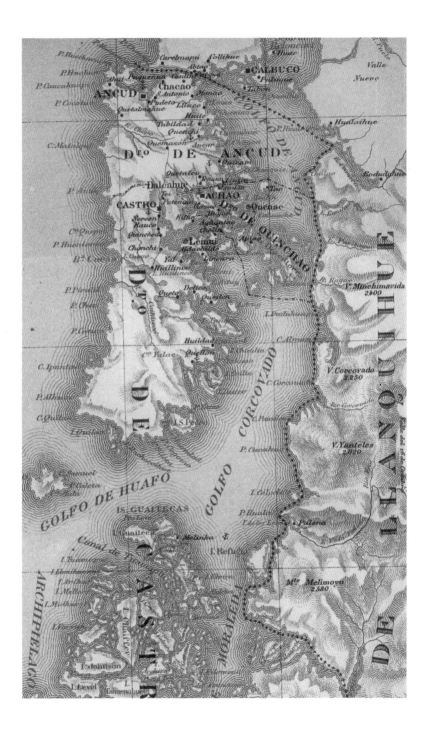

The island of Chiloé is notorious for a dank and macabre mythology in which much of the population is said to still believe: goblins, warlocks and all manner of creatures are thought to populate the caves in the forest along the eastern shore. When Darwin visited in the 1830s there were tales of people accused of devil worship being sent to the Inquisition in Lima. More than a century later Chatwin wrote of a *brujeria*, or witchcraft, sect rumoured to be flourishing in Chiloé, with the sole purpose of spreading evil and causing pain and misery to humankind. According to Chatwin they kept their headquarters in a cave near Quicavi, where the *Invunche*, or Guardian of the Cave, lives on human flesh and keeps the secrets of the Brotherhood safe.

Of the church in Castro, Darwin wrote that it *stands in the middle, is entirely built in plank, and has a picturesque and venerable appearance.* I wanted to see it for myself. From the town of Puerto Montt, in Chile's Los Lagos region, I hired a car and took a ferry to the island. The church had not long been declared a UNESCO World Heritage Site. Soaring beams of dark wood were joined in an aerial reflection of the loamy earth of the island. Figures of the Passion of Christ were suspended on its walls, each sheened with chipped lacquer. The Madonna showed her patriotism with two Chilean flags. The bleeding Jesus on Calvary was a wax anatomical model. In the playpark opposite the church I saw pigs rooting through broken bottles.

I camped on the beach between Quicavi and Tenaún, and lit a fire. Out of the darkness came the sound of galloping hooves; twinned pinpoints of red light danced around those sounds, speeding towards me. I switched on my torch, called out in a shaky voice, *Buenas tardes!* A Chilote on horseback appeared in the pallid beam; the two glowing eyes I'd seen were his concurrently smoked cigarettes. He didn't reply and, after glancing down at me with disdain, cantered on.

On the western coast of Chiloé I watched the Pacific.

The roar of it, the mother of all oceans, deadened all other sound. Wind whipped out of the fog, blowing the sand into a delicately dancing mist.

My mind couldn't begin to grasp the immensity of water: the same ocean lapping the Antarctic, California, the Aleutians, Kamchatka, Japan, Sumatra, New Zealand and countless thousands of atolls and islands sprinkled across the globe's half-span. From it, tropical sunshine raises clouds which pour rains over the whole of the earth. The numbers of dialects and languages spoken along these shores was inconceivable, as were the diversity and abundance of the species and habitats dipped in the water that slapped the soles of my feet. In my mind's eye I was returned to the childhood atlas, and its own map of the Pacific.

DISTANCES & TIMES BY STEAMER		
From	Naut. Miles	Transit in days
Brisbane to Vancouver	6876	23
San Francisco to Auckland	5924	18
" " Salina Cruz	2287	12
Shanghai to Vladivostok	1123	3½
Sydney to Hongkong	4913	28
" Melbourne	576	2
Valparaiso to Punta Arenas	1414	6
" Salina Cruz	3262	13
Wellington to Cape Horn	4614	14
Yokohama to Hongkong	1580	6
" San Francisco	5477	18
" Seattle	4259	16
" Vancouver	4280	12

George Philip & Son, Ltd.

Equatorial Scale 1: 70,000,000

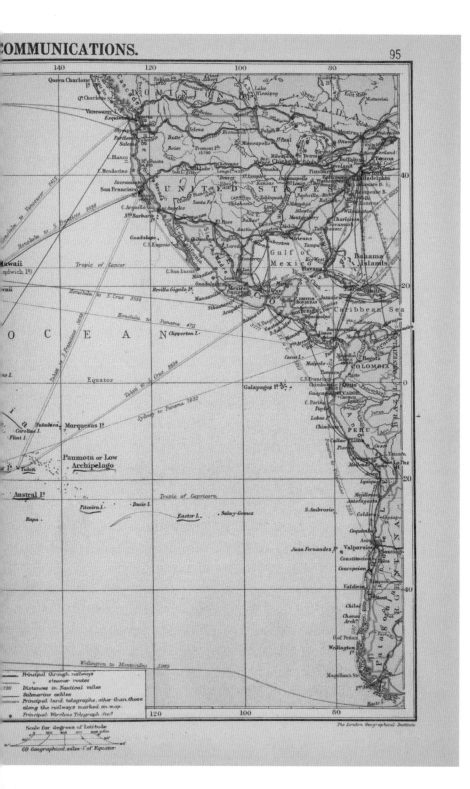

The road lay along a very broad beach, on which even after so many fine days, a terrible surf was breaking. I was assured that after a heavy gale, the roar can be heard even at Castro, a distance of no less than twenty-one sea miles across a hilly and wooded country . . .

Don Pedro asked the commandant to give us a guide to Cucao. The old gentleman offered to come himself; but for a long time, nothing would persuade him, that two Englishmen really insisted to go to such an out of the way place as Cucao.

CHARLES DARWIN

I realise that often in adult life I've considered books as portable islands, in the way they grant isolation from one's surroundings, offering relief from immediate demands and space for contemplation. *More and more, as we grow older . . . great novels declare their authority*, wrote Helen Dunmore. *They will certainly outlive us, like sea or rock or sand. We can inhabit their world for a while, and be changed by it, but they are forever moving beyond us to the next generation.*

I take refuge in prose as one might in a boat . . . I cross over to an island, and every time, the moment I read the first sentences, it is as if I were rowing far out on the water.

W.G. SEBALD

There was a time in my youth when, like Bruce Chatwin,
I was captivated by E. Lucas Bridges' *The Uttermost Part of the Earth* – a book about growing up on the island of Tierra del Fuego, at the tip of Patagonia. At twenty-six years old I went there, between a spell training in emergency medicine and taking up a job as a doctor with the British Antarctic Survey.

The town of Ushuaia was lined with backpackers' hostels where restless travellers idled, and asked one another for leads on finding a cheap passage to Antarctica. On the other side of the Beagle strait, named for Darwin's ship, Navarino and Hoste Islands came and went through the mist. Beyond them, I knew, stood Cape Horn, the full stop at the end of the Americas.

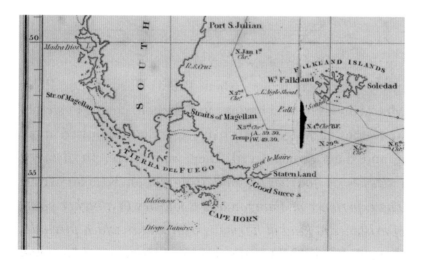

After a day or two I went north to the Valle Carbajal. Eagles watched warily from the low-hanging branches I passed along the trails, a Fuegian fox ran off with my bread rolls, but at the summit I swung my legs over glaciers the colour of petrified sky. In four days along the trails there were no other walkers.

You will find nothing there. There is nothing in Patagonia.

JORGE LUIS BORGES

In Patagonia the monotony of the plains, or expanse of low hills, the universal unrelieved greyness of everything, and the absence of animal forms and objects new to the eye, leave the mind open and free to receive an impression of nature as a whole.

W.H. HUDSON

For Borges, Patagonia was an absence. But even emptiness has its compensations: when Brian Keenan and John McCarthy were held hostage in Lebanon, chained together in a series of dungeons for five years, they fantasised about it and, later, when freed, they went there. In *Between Extremes: A Journey Beyond Imagination* Keenan wrote: *The experience of Patagonia is a journey to a higher plane of existence, a kind of harmony with nature which precludes thought.* But for McCarthy it proved too much: *I have had enough of the world's grand scale. The landscapes of*

Patagonia and Tierra del Fuego have disturbed me. It is like meeting some glamorous and beautiful character whom you wish to befriend but you cannot think how to open a conversation.

As ship's doctor on the Royal Research Ship *Ernest Shackleton* I sailed from England late one October for the Antarctic. In the two weeks it took to reach the equator we skirted the Isle of Wight, Madeira, the Canary Islands and the Cape Verde Islands. A further week's sailing took us past the archipelago of Fernando de Noronha and down the coast of Brazil to the Uruguayan capital of Montevideo.

A couple of days after leaving Montevideo the ship picked up some camp followers: nimble, black-browed albatrosses, perhaps relatives of that exile that turned up in Unst. We hadn't yet reached as far south as the latitudes of the wandering albatross, known to taxonomists as *Diomedea exulans*.

Off the Patagonian coast I rushed from below decks to my first view of the Falkland Islands, thirty days after leaving England. Low, defiant swells of land, fringed with beaches of gold, and behind them all a dark mountain the colour of military camouflage.

Falkland Islands

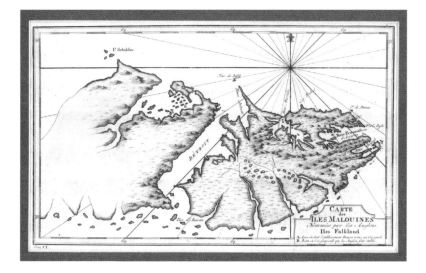

Linnaeus named the wandering albatross for the Greek warrior Diomedes who, in Dante's *Inferno*, compares the busy city of Florence to a vast bird whose wing-beats darken the earth, and whose name *spreads over hell*. The canto goes on to describe Ulysses's voyage south beyond the Pillars of Hercules, his ship's oars beating as wings, until a remote island rises before them beneath unfamiliar southern stars. The island is crowned with the dim mountain of Purgatory. Just before reaching it, Ulysses's ship is caught in a whirlpool, a maelstrom; *over us the booming billow clos'd.*

The Falkland Islands are purgatorial for some – military
staff consider it a misfortune to be posted there. But to me
the grandeur of ocean and sky there, the squall of the
natural world, the wind whipping up from Antarctica, all
granted the islands a sense of timelessness. I hiked out to
one of the beaches, mercifully cleared of the mines laid by
retreating Argentinian soldiers more than twenty years
before. Settling into a hollow, inches from gentoo penguins
on their nests, I coughed back the stench of guano, familiar
from Shetland, and fended off dive-bombing skuas.
Piebald Commerson's dolphins played in the shallows.
Europe felt distant, its history as thick as dust in a forsaken
library. I visited penguin rookeries, thriving with new life,
their layers of guano suggesting they'd been continuously
occupied for over two million years.

On our approach to South Georgia, the ship pushed through bands of fog and sunshine, the seas around the ship's hull teeming with life. Fur seals somersaulted through the water; sooty, wandering and black-browed albatrosses swooped in the ship's wake. The waves frothed with giant petrels, cape petrels and penguins.

From the ship I took a small boat, a 'tender', to be met on a jetty by scientists who lived year-round on Bird Island – a splinter of rock off South Georgia's western cape. They handed me a broom handle 'seal-bodger', with which I was to beat off any fur seals that approached with fangs bared.

Black-browed albatrosses nested along the slopes among the tussock grass. Up on the plateau I tiptoed, awe-struck, between the nests of wandering albatrosses. These immense birds, larger than swans and with a twelve-foot wingspan, were untroubled by my presence, marvellous in their serenity.

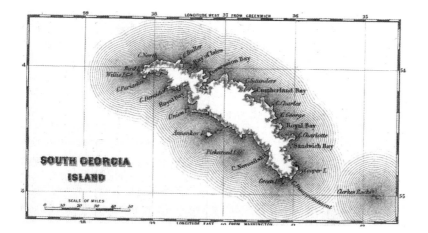

SOUTH GEORGIA
ISLAND

SCALE OF MILES
0   10   20   30   40   50

*At intervals it arched forth its vast archangel wings, as
if to embrace some holy ark. Wondrous flutterings and
throbbings shook it . . . Through its inexpressible, strange
eyes, methought I peeped to secrets which took hold of
God. As Abraham before the angels, I bowed myself.*

HERMAN MELVILLE

In South Georgia the longing was strong to lose oneself in
the mountains, to walk for days high in the ice, in timelessness, and see only rock faces, delicate shades of lilac and
crimson, the only focus point for the eye that of infinity.

*South
Orkney*

The South Orkney Islands lie almost due south of the
Falklands; they stand not on the latitude of their northern
namesakes, but on the equivalent distance from the equator to Shetland. The refrigerating effects of Antarctic
weather systems are so effective that, while the hills of
Shetland flourish in campion and thrift, the South Orkneys'
sole efflorescence is ice. In summer the beaches there teem
with penguins and seals, hauling themselves from the sea
as if in search of sanctuary.

To reach the remote Antarctic research station that
was to be my home for fourteen months the captain took
a long loop east of South Georgia, hoping to find a way
around the perpetually turning millstone of ice that abrades
the islands and sea floor of the Weddell Sea.

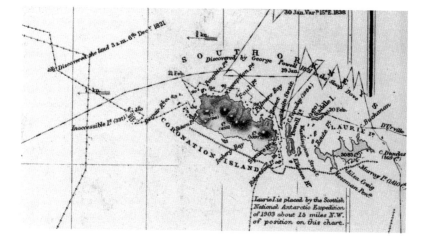

In heavy fog we passed within a few miles of the South
Sandwich Islands, an arc of active volcanoes over two
hundred miles long, five of which pour forth ceaseless
clouds of noxious, climate-modifying gas. I stood on the
deck sniffing the air for its hints of sulphur. One of the
sailors told me that mariners have been poisoned simply by
stepping ashore.

As we passed blindly within a few miles of these islands,
among the most remote in the world, I watched our
progress on the ship's satellite navigation system: a God's-
eye view of the broad arc of the archipelago, four hundred
kilometres long, as they snagged and set in rippling motion
our canopy of eastbound clouds.

South
Sandwich
Islands

89

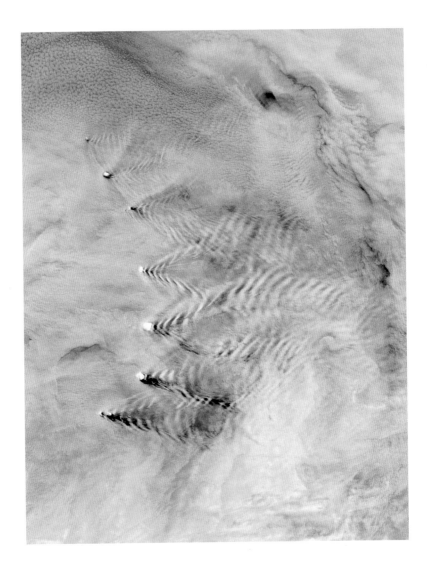

The association of islands with danger was well attested in the storybooks I read as a child. Take C.S. Lewis's *The Voyage of the Dawn Treader* in which the travellers encounter an island pool with the power to turn anything dipped into its waters to a deadly gold – a neat inversion of the association between islands and treasure. On another of Lewis's islands there's a dragon cave that leaks sulphurous smoke. *Most of us know what we should expect to find in a dragon's lair,* writes Lewis, *but Eustace had read only the wrong books.*

I was relieved to have been reading the right books.

ISLAND RETREATS

I HAVE A friend who used to be a sort of self-governing urban monk – strictly non-denominational. His own view was that it's unnecessary to take oneself off to distant, isolated lands in search of peace or a heightened sense of reverence. His own favoured location was a traffic island in the middle of one of Edinburgh's busiest junctions. He was in the habit of sitting there in meditation among the exhaust fumes. One day the police moved him on. They said he must be up to *no good*.

The primitive forms of the word *island* include *illond,* *yllond, yland, hylan* and *ile-land.* The prefixes vary, but are all of Germanic origin meaning *water,* or *watery*

place – suited as much to describe a peninsula as a piece of land surrounded on all sides by water. Coverdale's Bible, refracted into early modern English from the Hebrew, ascribed the word *Ilondes* to the entire Mediterranean coastline as populated by Gentiles. It was intended to take in those lands of Asia Minor, Greece and North Africa into which teemed the descendants of Japheth, as in this verse of Isaiah: *Let them give glory unto the LORD, and declare his praise in the islands.*

The *Oxford English Dictionary* asserts that by the seventeenth century the prefixes 'i', 'hy', 'ile', were 'erroneously' conflated with the French and Italianate 'isle', and by the 1600s the bastard word 'island' was becoming routine. In 1586 Sir Philip Sidney wrote of an Arcadian *iland within the lake*; by 1598 Hakluyt could write *Godred . . . tooke possession of the South part of the Island.*

The distinction is academic; that a peninsula may stand service as an island seems to me fair enough.

A year or so after Barra, approaching the winter solstice, I was assigned a fortnight away from my schedule of hospital work. A disintegrating love affair had sickened me, and none of my friends were free to travel. Between bouts of incapacitating sadness I made plans to travel to Greece.

The Athos peninsula is home to a complex of monasteries where, for a millennium, Orthodox Christians have gone on pilgrimage. I am not an Orthodox Christian, but had read that they'd welcome me nevertheless.

To reach the peninsula I'd be obliged to fly to Athens, take a night train north to Thessaloniki, then apply in the city office for a pilgrim's permit that would be valid at most for a week. With two weeks of leave, there was no hurry – there were even a few days to spare before it was necessary to depart for Athens.

On a whim I drove to Thurso, on the Arctic coast of Scotland, and took a ferry through dense solstice darkness to Orkney, an archipelago of forty or so islands, with the intention of reaching the remotest of them – North Ronaldsay. At that latitude, at that time of year, there were about five hours of light each day. There were only ten other passengers on the ferry. I walked off into freezing darkness, and my first view of Orkney was of the land between the towns of Stromness and Kirkwall. It was mid-morning, and the light was beginning to gather. Even in that semidarkness the landscape was soothing, not at all like Shetland or nearby Sutherland: a maze of silver inlets set between gently rolling peninsulas. So green, even in December. Kirkwall seemed like every small harbour town at first glance: a few little streets, a wide harbour perfumed by fish oil and diesel.

I was to reach North Ronaldsay by plane, as I'd missed the island's once-a-week ferry. The taxi driver who took me to the airport told me he could live on every island in Orkney but that one. *It is just too isolated*, he said.

The plane had room for only eight passengers. I was given a seat behind the pilot with a cockpit view as the

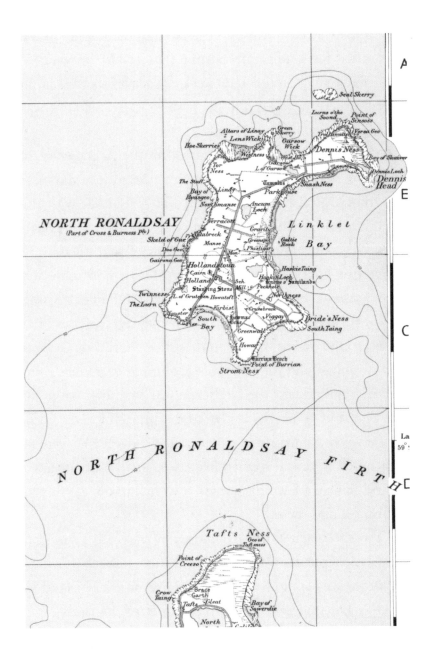

Seal Skerry

Lurns o'the Soond
Point of Sinsoss

Altars of Linay
Green Skerry
Trollavatten
Veran Geo

Lens Wick
Garsow Wick
Dennis Ness

Hoe Skerries
Westness
Wat Ho.
Bay of Skaiver

Tor Ness
Garsow
L. of Garson
Dennis Loch

The Staff
Jummin's
Snash Ness
Dennis Head

Bay of Ryasgeo
Lindy
Parkhouse

Northmanse
Ancum Loch

NORTH RONALDSAY
(Part of Cross & Burness Ph.)

Verracott

Gravits
Linklet

H<u>o</u>labreck
Greenspit
Galtie Rock
Bay

Skeld of Gue
Manse
Phuligar

Doo Geo

Gairsng Geo
Mon.
Haskie Taing

Hollandstoun
Hooking Loch

Cairn
Seh.
Mill.s
Senome o Samilands

Holland
Peckhole

Standing Stone
Nor Unness

Twinness
L. of Grutchen
Howatoft

The Lurn

Kirbist
Grimbreck

Leuster
South
Bay
Newmal
Bea
Viggay
Bride's Ness

Greenwall
South Taing

Howar

Garrian Broch
Pool of Burrian

Strom Ness

NORTH RONALDSAY FIRTH

Tafts Ness
Geo of Taft ness

Point of Creeso

Crow Taing
Brace Garth

Tafts
Cleat
Bay of Sowerdie

North

propellers roared and the plane jerked skywards as if tugged on marionette strings. Beneath me, perspective resolved into a living map, the heaving sea breaking along the coastlines of each island of the archipelago.

In the half-light of three circumpolar winter 'days' I walked circuits of North Ronaldsay (circumference: thirteen miles) until it was time to leave for Greece. Sixty people lived there alongside a couple of thousand sheep of a breed so primitive they are thought to have arrived on the island during the Iron Age. They have evolved to subsist on seaweed rather than grass – a talent almost unique, and shared with a single species of iguana resident in one of the Galapagos Islands. The only sounds were of wind and sea, the plane once a day, a tractor at about the same regularity and, near the guest house, the rotation of wind generators. Seals along the shore would belly-flop away from my approach; occasionally a young one, or one I had inadvertently cut off from the water, would turn and hiss at me. The seabirds were unusually fearless.

Given the abundance of sheep and of seals in North Ronaldsay I reasoned that, if marooned there, I'd hardly starve. On Juan Fernandez the original Robinson Crusoe, Alexander Selkirk, killed sea lions with relative ease:

Observing that though their Jaws and Tails were so terrible, yet the Animals being mighty slow in working themselves round, he had nothing to do but place himself exactly opposite to their middle, and as close to them as possible, and he despatched them with his Hatchet at will.

RICHARD STEELE

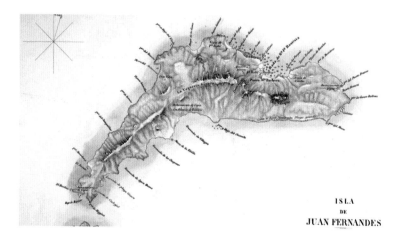

ISLA
DE
JUAN FERNANDES

On the twilit morning of my fourth day in North Ronaldsay I boarded the little aeroplane again, and flew over the mosaic of Orkney's northern isles to Kirkwall. To the north, through patches in the cloud, I thought I could discern a dull green glow in the sky – a 'quiet arc' of auroral light. From Kirkwall I took an empty bus to the port town of Stromness in the west of Orkney's Mainland, to join the ferry that would return me to the Scottish mainland. It was a six-hour drive to Edinburgh, where I'd catch my flight to Athens.

The sleeper from Athens threw me out onto the streets of Thessaloniki at 6.20 a.m. Before I could apply for a permit to visit Athos I needed a letter of introduction from the British consulate – a hutch of an office located partway up a concrete high-rise.

On its steps, facing towards the Mediterranean, waiting for the office to open, I read a memoir by a man who'd wintered alone in the high Arctic, *North to the Night* by Alvah Simon. He nearly lost his mind, yet his need to retreat into that isolation, and for that clear, polar air, was like his need for oxygen. From time to time I'd glance up at the Aegean's glitter glare, my mind spinning over an unmappable white wilderness.

The consul confirmed that I was not a criminal; I took her signed assurance to a pilgrims' office where three suavely efficient men behind stacks of buff-coloured files issued me with a *diamonitirion*, or permit for Athos. I'd sail there the next morning from Ouranoupoli, the 'City of Heaven'.

The shoreline at the City of Heaven felt rich and fertile after Orkney's blasted winter beaches. Even on the highest, stillest hillside, there was evidence of human industry.

The mountain itself was a conical fairy-tale peak, rising from the tip of a sinuous peninsula. A wasp's waist of land connected the peninsula to the mainland, interrupted by the remains of an ancient canal named for an emperor of Persia, but the roads were inaccessible – the only way in was by boat.

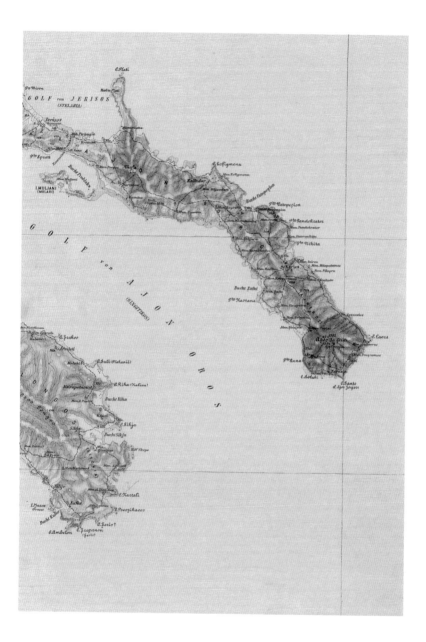

From the boat I watched dolphins leap ahead of the bow, and avoided the chatter and cigarette smoke of monks returning from furlough in the city. On arrival at the administrative hub, Karyes, the monks fled into waiting jeeps. Though I raised my thumb and asked around for a lift to the Great Lavra monastery, none offered. I was left standing in the dust with Francesco, a spry Italian convert to Orthodoxy, who informed me he was now on his tenth visit to the peninsula. Hitching a lift was unlikely, he said, and I should instead accompany him on foot to the nearby monastery of Iviron.

I became Orthodox after reading The Way of a Pilgrim, he said, a book about a Russian serf's spiritual awakening that was discovered earlier last century buried in a library in a monastery on Athos. Its fame in English translation was broadened by the approval of J.D. Salinger, who has one of his characters, a young woman called Franny, follow its advice to *pray without ceasing*.

It's a good read, Francesco said, *as long as you ignore all that Slavic sentimentality*. As part of his wanderings, the pilgrim journeys to a monastery on Solovetsky Island in the White Sea.

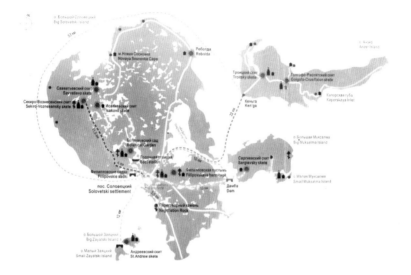

So here I am at the present time, stealing off to the solitary ascetic retreat in the Solovetsky Monastery in the White Sea . . . about which I have heard on good authority that it is a most suitable place for the contemplative life.

THE WAY OF A PILGRIM

The love affair I'd left behind still felt as close as the pulse in my throat. Several times a day squalls of sorrow, or anxiety, or regret, would throw me off balance. I resolved to commit those gusts of emotion to the paper of an ever-lengthening letter, to corral them in ink instead of letting them shriek around my head. *When I get back*, I thought, *I'll post it to her.*

Jean-Jacques Rousseau, famous for his belief that human beings are *born free, but everywhere live in chains*, held a passionate belief in the therapeutic value of being able to wander freely. His last book, *Reveries of the Solitary Walker*, was based on a series of ten walks in which he meditated on his life, his mistakes and the many roads to wisdom. Happiness, he says, had come to him most powerfully when he sought refuge for two months on the lake-island of St Peter in Switzerland.

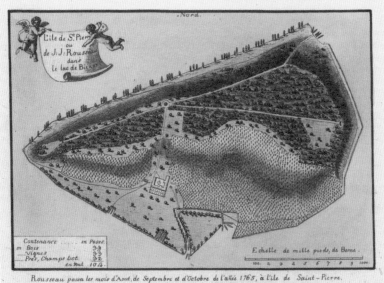

.Nord.

L'île de St Pierre
ou
de J. J. Rousseau
dans
le lac de Bienne

Contenance ..... en Poses.
en Bois   39
Vignes   33
Prés, Champs &ct.   32
en tout 104

Echelle de mille pieds de Berne.

Rousseau passa les mois d'Aout, de Septembre et d'Octobre de l'añée 1765, à l'île de Saint-Pierre.
il en partit le 24 Octobre.

The happiness Rousseau felt on St Peter's isle was a consequence of the simplicity of his life there: he had few of his possessions, an abundance of leisure and the conversation of just a handful of others. He used an Italian phrase to describe this kind of happiness: there was a deep joy in *far niente* – 'doing nothing' – a joy that came more easily on an island that provided some distance from distraction. The island curtailed the possibilities of engaging with others, and the connections he felt were all the deeper and more satisfying as a result.

I know men will be careful not to give me back such a sweet refuge when they did not want to leave me there, Rousseau wrote of the island. *But at least they will not prevent me from transporting myself there each day on the wings of my imagination.*

Like a fortress, the monastery of Iviron lay banked into
the hillside, high and grey, its tiny windows were archers'
slots. The building was a thousand years old; its cobbled
track felt rutted with history. It led to a wide courtyard,
enclosed by open, iron-cased doors. I was greeted in the
Archontariki, the pilgrims' reception, by a quiet monk
with an Australian accent who exchanged pleasantries,
in English, about my hospital work. He offered me
Turkish delight – claimed as a cultural tradition of both
Greeks and Turks, and a reminder that for much of the
last five hundred years the Athos peninsula was under
Ottoman rule.

The office of vespers was about to begin. I was expected to attend but was asked, as an unbeliever, to stand outside the church. A fat monk told me to turn my back so that I couldn't see the others at prayer. For two hours I stood in the half-light, listening to the monks' chants and responses. Dinner was a bowl of rice with cauliflower stew; the candles in the dormitory were extinguished at 7 p.m.

It's said that for a thousand years there have been no women permitted on Athos. There's no radio or television, prayer is obligatory between three and five times a day. The monks eat simple food. They have no money.

Herman Melville noted the same in the Marquesas:

No foreclosures of mortgages, no protested notes,
no bills payable, no debts of honour; no poor relations . . .
no destitute widows . . . no beggars; no debtors' prison,
no proud and hard-hearted nabobs in Typee; or to sum
up all in one word – no money!

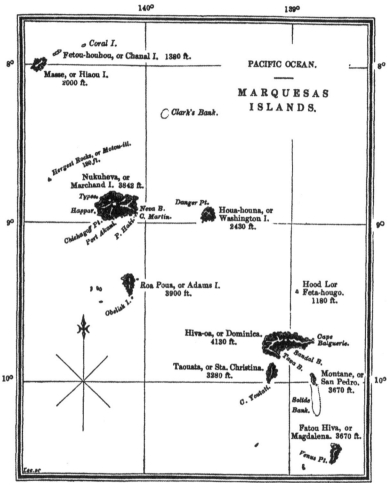

Coral I.

Fetou-houbou, or Chanal I. 1380 ft.

Masse, or Hiaou I.
2000 ft.

PACIFIC OCEAN.

MARQUESAS
ISLANDS.

Clark's Bank.

Hergest Rocks, or Motou-iti.
180 ft.

Nukuheva, or
Marchand I. 3842 ft.

Typee.

Happar.

Neva B.
C. Martin.

Danger Pt.

Houa-houna, or
Washington I.
2430 ft.

Chichagoff Pt.

Port Akaui

P. Hahi

Roa Poua, or Adams I.
3900 ft.

Obelisk I.

Hood I. or
Feta-hougo.
1180 ft.

Hiva-oa, or Dominica.
4130 ft.

Cape
Balguerie.

Sandal B.

Taouata, or Sta. Christina.
3280 ft.

Tava B.

Montane, or
San Pedro.
3670 ft.

C. Youtati.

Solide
Bank.

Fatou Hiva, or
Magdalena. 3670 ft.

Venus Pt.

Lee.sc

140° Long. West of Greenwich.

In an essay by Kathleen Jamie I read of her relief at being released from distractions and responsibilities to simply watch the sea. And with the monks of Athos I began to wonder if being bathed day after day, year after year, in the sounds and light of the sea, had the power to evoke kindness. But being so isolated, the monks had fewer opportunities to practise compassion than if they'd stayed in their home communities.

The idea of holiness clings to the Shiants, as to other islands. Remoteness from the world looks like a closeness to God and intriguingly, it turns out that the association of islands and holiness predates anything Christian.

ADAM NICOLSON

In the courtyard of the Great Lavra monastery cement mixers were going, chainsaws were buzzing at firewood, hammers were being struck on stone. There was the sound of a generator off beyond the solar panels. Vegetable gardens had been staked out to the west, as well as greenhouses. On a bench there I met Dimitri, who'd left a job in Lausanne to return to Greece, do his military service, and find God.

He told me about a doctor he knew who'd found work as an emergency physician in Italy. This doctor had felt exhausted and sick after every shift, and wondered if he was absorbing all the pain and suffering of his patients. He decided to stop thinking with his intellect, and allow his decisions to emerge in some indefinable way from *the heart.* If his heart didn't offer a preference between two paths then he would decline to make the decision.

He quit his job in Italy, returned to Greece and found work in a quiet island practice. Ever since, Dimitri said, this man had enjoyed something close to enlightenment. *He felt in perfect harmony with his life and with the world around him*, he added.

I skirted the Athos mountainside along a thin, ancient track. In places it had worn into a holloway two metres deep. The leaves were autumnal, and there was a thick, luscious silence broken only by the sound of bees, falling water and, close to some of the smaller retreats, donkey bells.

As I sat overlooking an Aegean panorama, scribbling at my letter, an old monk leading a donkey passed me, fat and happy, muttering in Greek. He insisted on tying my rucksack to his donkey, motioning for me to walk ahead of him. He had thick untied boots and wild hair; several frayed army jackets flapped in layers at his breast. For an hour I walked ahead of him through the forests, feeling grateful for losing the weight of my pack, walking slowly for the sake of the donkey. At a spring I filled my mug and offered it to the monk; he grinned and downed the mugful in one, droplets shining in his beard.

I was relieved when he and his donkey turned away down a track, because it meant I could stop again as I pleased, and sit in solitude once more.

Sometimes the monks of Athos seemed like members of a subdued boys' club, and I wondered that they could dedicate their lives to such relinquishing, such denial, of family life. At those moments their impractical, flowing robes and ceremonial hats appeared ridiculous, as did all their absurd chanting and bell-ringing. Then the apparent peace of such a life overwhelmed me.

To approach these humorous and kindly men, the monks of Mount Athos, in a temper of psychological understanding, it is necessary to forswear, if only temporarily, the sting of these prejudices. Let the humanist realise, atheist though he be, that the religious seeks, after all, only the same as himself by other roads.

ROBERT BYRON

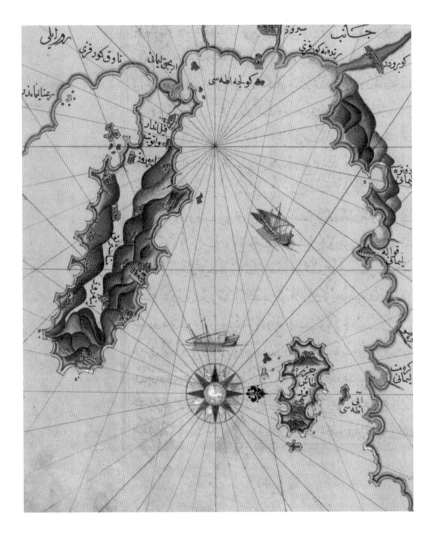

On the walls of the next monastery to welcome me, Gregoriou, I sat watching the incandescent sea, feeling the strength of the sun's heat. The anguished letter was spending less and less time out of my backpack. My additions to it were getting shorter.

Inside the pilgrims' quarters I found an empty storage room with mattresses and blankets, a radiator and a window. The room was situated directly over the boat-house runway. My sleep was suffused with the drawl of shingle and the melodies of water in motion.

I was taken to see the one monk in the monastery who spoke English. Father Damianos was ironing bed sheets in a high room looking out over the bay. He appeared younger than his forty years. Expressions flitted swiftly over his face as he spoke. He was a Cypriot from south London, with blue eyes between his Orthodox cap and thick black beard. He made me coffee, and as he pressed bed sheets, we talked.

He'd been travelling the world through his early thirties, he said, searching for something without knowing what. His brother suggested they coincide in Greece, and together they determined, on a whim, to visit Athos. The first monastery the men came to was Gregoriou. They stayed first for a week *to get used to the new rhythm*. His brother left. Damianos extended his stay to a month, then four months. Then he became a novice.

After three years in Gregoriou, Damianos felt he had to go back into the world, to confirm his knowledge of what he'd be giving up were he to commit to monastic life. He visited a Catholic monastery in the south of England where he met an Anglican nun sent there by her psychologist following a nervous breakdown. That a nun should seek the attentions of a clinical psychologist for what amounted to a spiritual crisis demonstrated, he insisted, the incongruities inherent in the Western tradition, and he returned to Gregoriou and took his vows. That encounter had been four years previously. He had yet to visit any other monasteries on Athos.

He was convinced that death is the culmination of our lives, and in some ways is our life's reason. That it is only a door.

I saw only two dawns at the Athonite ascetics' retreat of St Anne – each arrived as the two-hour ceremony of matins came to a close. Sunlight approached in great arches from the horizon, bridging the night. After a breakfast of bread and olives I sat in the blue light; sounds were again of donkey bells, waterfalls, birds singing. The chapels clinging to the mountainside, the forest, the glittering sea, all proffered the palpable presence of . . .

. . . of what? I couldn't define how it felt, but only that ease of mind was in its gift.

But it was clear that, as in Iona, my redemption lay elsewhere.

In Athens I reread the lengthening letter and, with a great sense of liberation, dropped it into a municipal bin.

The poet Nancy Campbell describes a winter she spent in the small Greenlandic island of Upernavik, north of the Arctic Circle. There's a settlement there of a thousand or so people, a museum and a shop. There are many icebergs, and occasional polar bears. Once every month a Frenchman *whose name and history no one knew* would arrive by boat from an even more remote island, where he lived alone. He would stock up wordlessly on a few essentials in the village store, before getting into his boat and motoring off into the labyrinth of islands and icebergs.

I heard similar stories on my own journeys along Greenland's coast, and wondered at the silence of that life, the clock of the waves beating time upon the shores of the Davis Strait. At what might have happened to this Frenchman to make such solitude necessary. His monthly visits to the shop, at least, sustained some kind of connection to the current of mankind. I wondered if he'd be missed when he stopped coming.

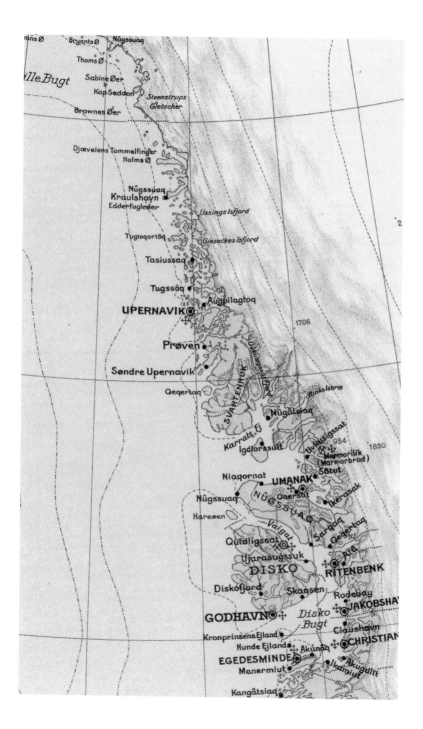

I wondered too if that Frenchman in Greenland, so steeped in his isolation, knew of John Donne's phrase *No man is an island*, from *Devotions Upon Emergent Occasions*. If he knew of the philanthropy expressed in the line *Any man's death diminishes me, because I am involved in mankind* – a sentiment that could stand as a maxim for the practice of medicine.

At the beginning of his isolation on Juan Fernandez Island Alexander Selkirk was harassed day and night by rats. To fend them off he tamed some semi-feral cats by offering them milk from the wild goats that he had captured, lamed and trapped in enclosures. On his return to Britain he reported that throughout his time on the island his greatest terror was that he'd die alone, and his body would be gnawed by rats and cats alike.

On Mount Athos I asked an old monk if he'd ever tried living in the desert.

No, he replied. *In the Bible it says it's not good for a man to be alone.* And then he grinned.

The Stoic philosopher and Roman emperor Marcus Aurelius didn't think it wise to go searching for peace beyond the confines of the self. *Nowhere can man find a quieter, or more untroubled retreat than in his own soul*, he said. Of Athos, he wrote: *Asia, Europe, are but nooks in the universe, the ocean a drop – Mount Athos a clod – time a point in eternity, alike little, fleeting, perishable.*

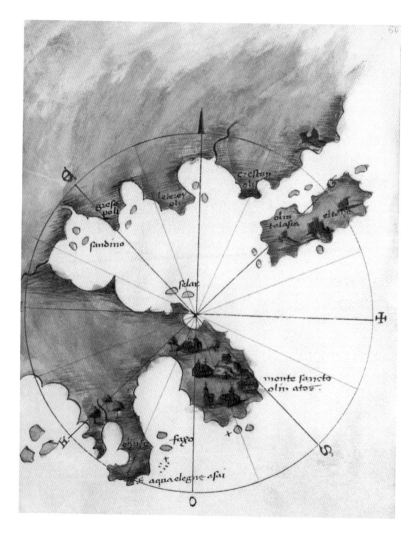

If a clod be washed away by the sea, Europe is the less.

JOHN DONNE

Forty years or so after Selkirk was marooned, four Russians were beached on Edge Island, in the Svalbard archipelago of the high Arctic. They survived for six years using arrowheads made of nails found in driftwood, and eating their prey raw. To counter scurvy in a land without vegetables they drank the blood of reindeer and foxes. One of their number who baulked at the drinking of blood died of that disease.

On their return to civilisation the three surviving men had lost their appetite for both alcohol and bread.

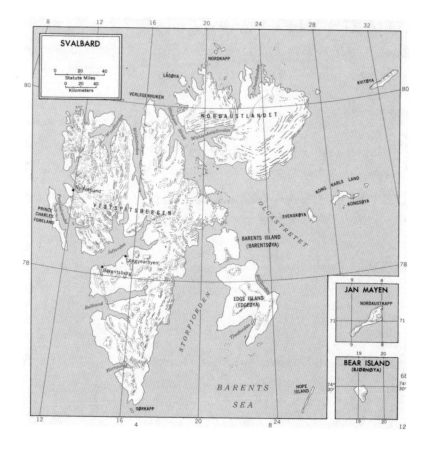

SVALBARD

0 20 40
Statute Miles
0 20 40
Kilometers

NORDKAPP
LÅGØYA
VERLEGENHUKEN
KVITØYA

NORDAUSTLANDET
Wahlenbergfjorden

VESTSPITSBERGEN

Ny-Ålesund

PRINCE
CHARLES
FORELAND

KONG KARLS LAND
KONGSØYA
OLGASTRETET
SVENSKØYA

BARENTS ISLAND
(BARENTSØYA)

Isfjorden
Longyearbyen
Barentsburg

EDGE ISLAND
(EDGEØYA)

JAN MAYEN
NORDAUSTKAPP

STORFJORDEN

Bellsund

Hornsund

BARENTS

SEA

HOPE
ISLAND

SØRKAPP

BEAR ISLAND
(BJØRNØYA)

From the little settlement of Longyearbyen, the capital of the Svalbard archipelago, I once sailed on a Russian icebreaker to see Spitsbergen's northern coast and Moffen Island – a flat disc of shingle, the last stop before the North Pole, and home to innumerable walruses and birds.

A little further along the coast was the place where Christiane Ritter, an Austrian painter, lived for a year in a trapper's hut between 1934 and 1935. In her book, *A Woman in the Polar Night*, she wrote: *We are seized by an uncontrollable longing for remote places. We want to go further and further into the Arctic lands, the islands in the ice, the frozen earth which is still lying there as on the day that God created it. Europe, and everything that binds us to Europe, is forgotten.*

The passage of Marcus Aurelius's *Meditations* that mentions Athos goes on to reflect on the nature of isolation and connectedness. *Bethink thee how all things are united*, it says, *part and parcel of, and connected with each other, whether through community of purpose, or similarity of form.*
Isolation, from this perspective, is an illusion.

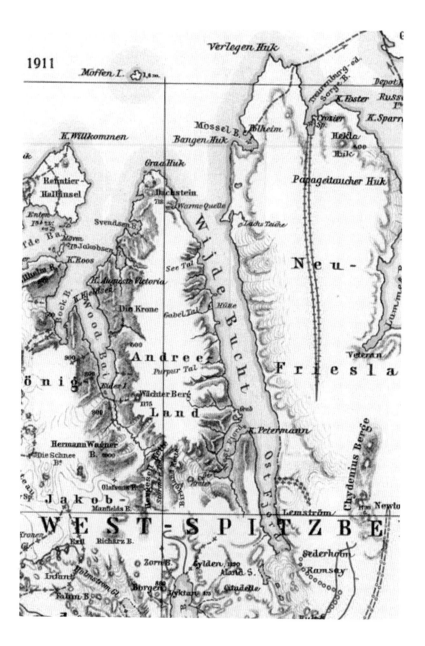

THE FORTUNATE ISLES

FROM THE VISITOR book of the hostel adjacent to the Faroe Islands' airport, a Dutchwoman's reflections on being trapped by the weather:

As distance can be an important factor in dreams, the Faroes have always presented a different world for me. Visiting them and experiencing the rapidly changing weather is the realisation of this dream.

St Brendan likely reached the Faroe Islands in his little leather boat sometime in the sixth century. Norse annals record that when the Vikings came to Faroe three hundred years later they found small communities of Irish monks still living there. There is little trace of them now, though the sheep native to the islands, a breed only recently extinct, are thought to have originated in Bronze Age Ireland.

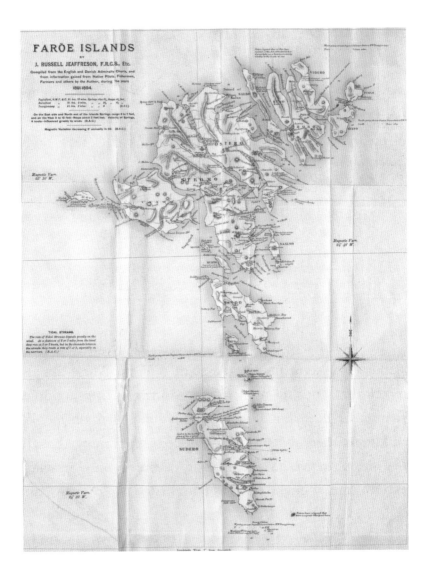

FARÖE ISLANDS

BY

J. RUSSELL JEAFFRESON, F.R.G.S., Etc.

Compiled from the English and Danish Admiralty Charts, and
from information gained from Native Pilots, Fishermen,
Farmers and others by the Author, during the years
1891-1894.

The slopes of the Faroes are so steep that I mostly had to pitch my tent lopsided, the poles at an eccentric angle. But it was usually possible to position the groundsheet over a flattened sheep track, just wide enough for my shoulders, so that when I lay down to sleep I didn't roll downhill. In the mornings I'd lie propped up in my tent with the flaps open, watching the light change over the waters of the north Atlantic. It was summer when I visited: at midnight it was still light enough to read.

It's an invigorating feeling to wake alone high on a hillside when no one else knows where you are. In the mornings I'd sit out, feeling the sun's heat smoking through the mist over the sea, and aspire to a whole life of casual wanderings, awakenings atop high cliffs, the whole clichéd Romantic dream. *There is a pleasure in the pathless woods, / There is a rapture on the lonely shore.* Gradually the haar would lift, and the sun's heat become gently offset by a breeze. My only companions were swarms of thick-bodied flies who danced between the blades of grass. Sometimes they landed on my hair; when I brushed them off they landed fat and dazed on the ground. The sea's ceaseless murmuring was hypnotic; the world felt good.

This mania for northern islands, and the exploration of Uummannaq their history, took me on past the Faroes to Iceland, and as far as the west coast of Greenland, where I camped on a small knuckle of rock with a bunch of international volunteers who were restoring an old mission building. The island was a few hours by boat from the capital, Nuuk, at the confluence of three immense fjords, and was called Uummannaq ('heart-shaped'), resembling not the cleft curves of a Valentine heart, but a fist-like knot of flesh.

On the summit of this island too I slept alone through sunlit nights, as I had in the Faroes. Work on the mission house was slow, and with the other volunteers I passed idyllic afternoons hooking the trout that swam in lazy shoals around the island, whittling from driftwood the forms of whale, seal and human. It was the human forms that were the hardest, that seemed to fit least well to the shapes of the wood, and of the land.

The International Court of Justice in The Hague decided the ownership of Greenland – the world's largest island – in 1933. This was a period in which the opinions of Greenlanders themselves were of little consequence. It is such a vast land – no wonder the Danes, with their love of rural spaces, lobbied fiercely for their right to ownership. The enormity of the place was an intoxication – its emptiness, its vast cordilleras of unclimbed peaks, deep with what was then thought of as unmelting snow.

Its snows are melting now, revealing immense mineral reserves – the world's largest Treasure Island.

GRÖNLAND
1: 5 000 000

DANMARK

GEODÆTISK INSTITUT

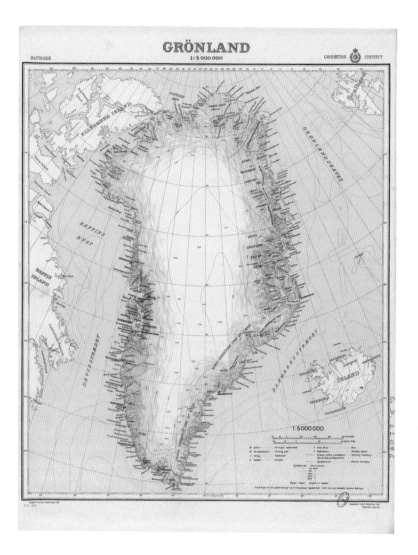

One of our Greenlandic guides, Ulrik, told me that I was the first Scotsman to set foot on his island. He added that I brought good karma. *Scots have a good attitude,* he said; *like us Greenlanders, you know how to drink.*

That was the evening one of the volunteers called Uummannaq a 'Paradise Island', as we hefted the codfish we'd caught and walked back to camp for dinner, the mountains majestic around us, the icebergs cracking and melting in the fjord, images to commit to memory, though they seemed more dream than reality. When I slept, I dreamt of whales spouting and diving in loops around the island.

The mist slid in and out of the fjords, webs of gossamer drifting between the mountains. One day a tourist group of ten Danes arrived in a chartered boat. They jumped ashore, looked at the old church, and at us in our squalor and happiness. I was sitting in the rain whittling sticks to make a dish-drying rack. I said to one of the women that it was a shame they had to rush away, and she replied, *But that's always the way with travelling, isn't it?* as if trying to convince herself.

Utopia

With his *Utopia* Thomas More inspired a whole genre of fantasy islands. On his island men and women worked equally, the days were fully occupied in practical tasks, and there were no locks on the doors.

On Uummannaq too, men and women worked equally, we were busy with practical tasks, and there were no locks.

The absence of locks was a convention I'd also noticed in Svalbard, but there the custom had developed to facilitate escape from roving polar bears.

A map of the world that does not include Utopia is not even worth glancing at, for it leaves out the one country at which Humanity is always landing. And when Humanity lands there, it looks out, and, seeing a better country, sets sail.

OSCAR WILDE

In 1360 a Franciscan friar from Oxford, enamoured of island journeys, is recorded as having toured alone the western shore of Greenland into the high Arctic. His account, titled *Inventio Fortunata* or 'fortunate discoveries', was delivered to his king in England. The book is lost, but for centuries his description influenced European maps of the north; echoes of his words appear on charts throughout the fifteenth and sixteenth centuries. The friar described a high mountain of magnetic stone at the North Pole, surrounded by whirlpool seas and four immense and roughly congruent islands. A priest who met this friar in Greenland claimed that *He journeyed further through the whole of the North, and put into writing all the wonders of the islands.* This priest's story was only recorded because a Dutch traveller happened to overhear him at the court of the Norwegian king.

Gerardus Mercator, the great Dutch cartographer, relates in a marginal note to his world map of 1569 that this priest *was descended in the fifth generation from those whom Arthur had sent to inhabit these lands.*

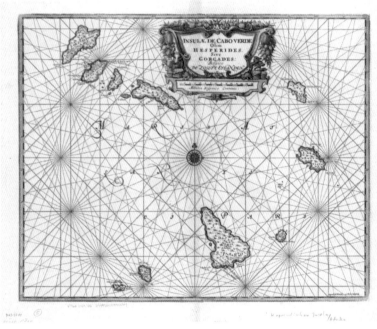

Given the place of islands in origin myths it's understandable that Mercator brings in King Arthur and his magical island, Avalon, which means *the place of apple trees*. Like the Greek Islands of the Blessed, it was guarded by an enchantress.

The Fortunate Isles or Hesperides of antiquity have been variously interpreted as the Canaries, Azores or Cape Verde – groups of islands standing out in the Atlantic, beyond the Pillars of Hercules but within the reach of Greek navigators. The Greek for 'fortunate isles' is *makárōn nêsoi*, granting all these quite separate archipelagos the unlovely designation *Macaronesia*.

In the 1300s Norse influence was waning and the English were on the lookout for new trade opportunities. I like to think of this Franciscan navigator, sent by his king to scope out alliances, losing sight of his original objective. With no vessel of his own, the journey from the British Isles to Greenland may have taken several years. In each community the friar would have had to work for his keep. Perhaps in Greenland's north he fell in among Inuit hunters. Like Nancy Campbell's Frenchman who turned up at the Upernavik store once a month, he seems to have welcomed the chance to put a few hundred miles of sea between himself and the problems of Europe.

Many would consider such a journey a penance, but the title of his book, *Inventio Fortunata*, suggests the opposite.

Elsewhere in myth, the Hesperides were the daughters of evening, located in the far west at the setting of the sun. Their father was Hesperus, the evening star, and their work was to guard the tree of life and its golden fruit.

Some place the Garden of Eden in the east, close to the confluence of the Tigris and Euphrates, but there exists an alternative tradition that places it among the islands to the west.

One Fortunate Isle was the fabulous Elixœa, of the Hyperboreans, where the stars, exhausted by their traverse of the heavens, would sink to rest, and where according to Plutarch the moon flew so near that one could easily distinguish the irregularities of its surface.

A traditional Gaelic folk charm, from the islands between Scotland and Ireland: *May I be an island in the sea, may I be a hill on the land, may I be a star when the moon wanes, may I be a staff to the weak one: I shall wound every man, no man shall wound me.*

ISLANDS *in the* SKY

FROM THE TOWN of Arica, on the Atacama Desert coast, the road climbed into the Andes through air that grew noticeably thinner, colder. Scattered scrub turned to stunted grasses. There were wide plains of terracotta and ochre; river gorges ribbed the valley. Quechua fortifications hung on the mountainsides like martins' nests, protecting hidden oases – the valley walls were still busy with terraces centuries after their construction. Three kilometres above sea level, maize thrived beside cacti and broad beans.

High over the Altiplano the sky was indigo, violet and a thunderous, forbidding blue – as if bruised by the extraordinary reach of the land. A small gap in the canopy to the west allowed an updraught of sulphurous yellows and oranges. Lightning flickered through the thin air in the narrow space between cloud and plain. It was mesmerising – a new landscape for me, previously unimagined.

Lake Titicaca was yet higher, almost four kilometres up, yet above it were more kingdoms of clouds: plumes of cumulus gathered and ran eastwards like billowed spinnakers. Over the course of each day they piled in heaps upon

one another before collapsing, at the same time every evening, in a frenzy of fantastical, pyrotechnical lightning. Beneath these thunderstorms squatted the islands of the sun and moon, where Quechua legend holds that the world was born.

An old Inca road skirted the lake, passing under a cave-shrine to Santa Maria Dolorosa. Then it climbed gently through long-abandoned terraces and over a summit, before dropping into a fertile valley. *Isla del Sol*

Boats were for hire at the shoreline; with three companions I rowed across the glittering lake towards the Isla del Sol – the island of the sun – our course parallel to the imaginary line on the lake dividing Bolivia from Peru. Fiery light played over the Isla de la Luna and the Cordillera Real to the east. Ashore, little boys at the jetty pointed to a hostel high on the hill, where a veranda faced out over the darkening waters of Titicaca. As I sat on the veranda that evening happiness rose in me, rich and sweet, with the rising of the moon. As in Lamu, the island seemed to offer respite from the chaotic and exhausting business of travelling on the mainland.

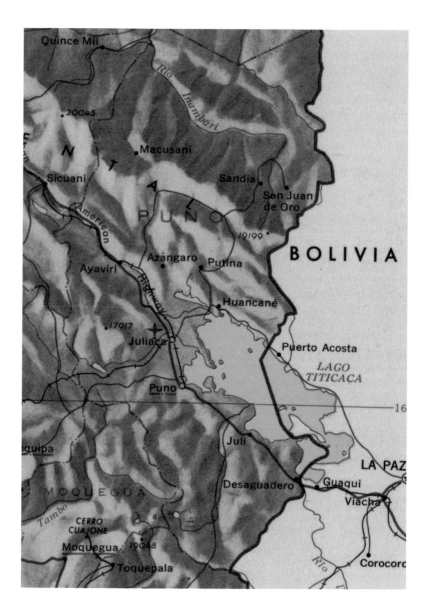

The beach was a gentle slope of sand, and next morning
I walked slowly into the lake until it reached my neck.
The water was cool and smooth, a dazzling mirror reflect-
ing the ferocity of the sun.

That night an Australian woman in the hostel became
unwell with altitude sickness. The owners crowded round
her: plump, bustling women in bright Bolivian homespun,
flashing their gold teeth and clicking their tongues.

When they heard I was a doctor they brought me a box,
in it a cache of drugs discarded by passing Westerners over
years: asthma inhalers, antihistamines, vitamins, antibiotics. I
explained the usage and dosage of each and waited while,
with great solemnity, my translated explanations were written
out on a card. After we'd been through them all the box and
explanations were tucked away like a chest of treasure.

The next morning the Australian woman took a ferry
to the mainland, then a bus to La Paz, and flew home.

The floating islands of the Uros are built of reeds moored close to the marshland where the distinction between earth and water is blurred. They were constructed, like Venice, as a refuge from violence on the mainland. Several small reed-islands had been set adrift on Titicaca for the benefit of tourists like me. Cruise boats passed ceaselessly, announced by megaphone-toting guides, their engines a buzzing in the brain.

From the Uros it was another two-and-a-half-hour voyage to the island of Taquile: again the slow, hypnotic whisper of the waves, stacks of cumulus tumbling towards the margins of the lake, and between those clouds, diapasons of light.

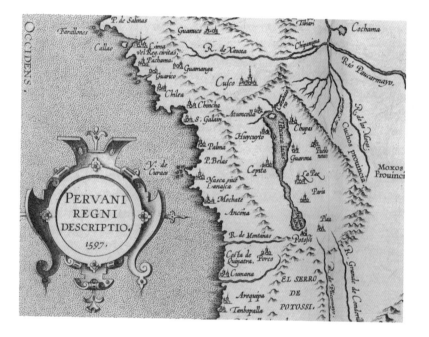

PERVANI REGNI DESCRIPTIO. 1597.

Two thousand years ago Pliny wrote in his monumental *Natural History* that *In Lydia, the islands named Calaminæ are not only driven about by the wind, but may be even pushed at pleasure from place to place, by poles.* Some of these floating islands could move in time to music, said Pliny, while others arranged themselves into geometrical shapes *so as at one time to exhibit the figure of a triangle and at another of a circle; but they never form a square.*

For this Annie Dillard called him *credulous Pliny.*

Taquile Island: a world separated by water, language, culture and disposition. Steep-sided as a fortress, terraces like contour lines, each thick with carefully tended maize, beans and potatoes.

From the ferry landing five hundred steps climbed to the top of the island, at an altitude of nearly 14,000 feet. I panted up them, struggling in the thin air, to be met by a grave trio – the head man atop a pedestal to make him higher than the other two. I paid him ten soles (about three US dollars), and was led by a boy through the maze of terraces to my allocated family. Tourists, as a valuable resource, were shared out equally between members of the community.

Thin tracks worn into trenches were woven like textiles into the island's earth; there were no roads, cars, dogs or electricity. 'My' house was built of mud bricks, but the bed and sheets were clean and the mattress covered with polythene against infestations. I ate by candlelight, and when I went to pay for the meal, saw that the family's wealth was held in an unlocked drawer beneath my place at the table.

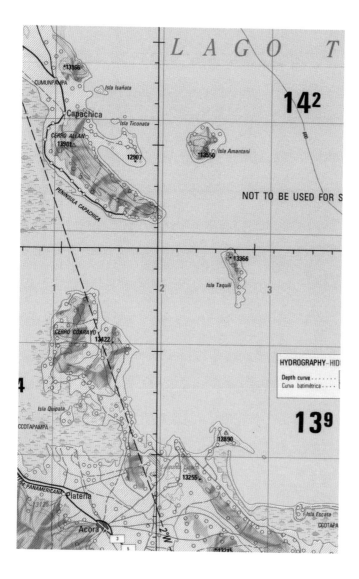

GULL ISLAND

THE BBC RADIO show *Desert Island Discs*, in which public figures are asked to nominate eight pieces of music they'd take to a desert island, has been running since January 1942. Its theme tune, accompanied by the sound of gulls calling, hasn't changed since its inception, and its popularity shows no sign of waning. The introduction to a book celebrating seventy years of the show observed *there was nothing new in asking people to nominate their favourite records: what really made the programme unique was the desert island . . . This was it: there was no going back to the record shop. Your choices defined you.*

Is that the perennial appeal of Crusoe? That we all have a thirst to define ourselves in solitude? That we dream of being castaways at last?

In my late twentics, training as a junior neurosurgeon in a particularly onerous hospital job in which I rarely saw natural light and struggled to meet the needs of the broken people admitted under my care, I began to think again about the Isle of May – the island I'd watched blinking in the night as a child through the window of a caravan awning. I learned that it was still a national nature reserve

Isle of May

for nesting seabirds. In the Old Norse of the Vikings, who subdued and then settled this coast over a thousand years earlier, May means *Gull Island: Maa-Øya*.

I made some phone calls, wrote an application letter, and a couple of months later found myself living in the island's terrace of lighthouse-keepers' cottages. My neighbours were a handful of ornithologists working for the Centre for Ecology and Hydrology, two Scottish Natural Heritage wardens, and several hundred thousand puffins, guillemots, razorbills, kittiwakes, herring gulls, great and lesser black-backed gulls, eiders, wagtails, chiffchaffs, warblers and wheatears. A great skua made predatorial, gangster-like circuits of the island. Gannets on stately fly-bys passed to and from the Bass Rock.

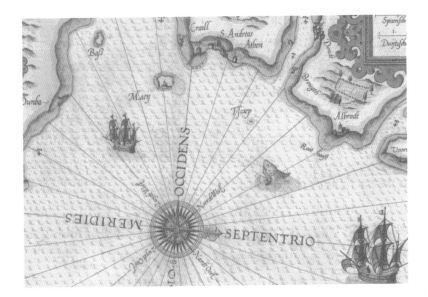

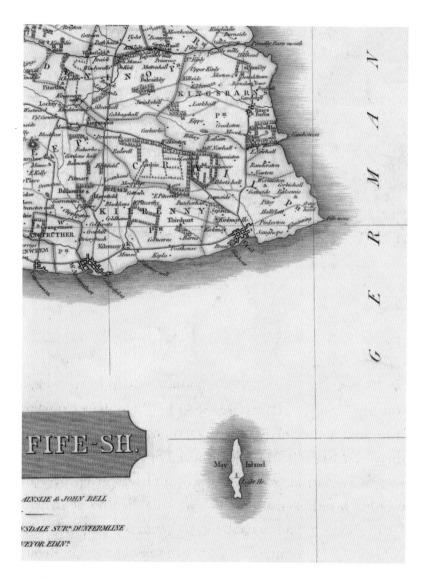

FIFE-SH.

AINSLIE & JOHN BELL

SDALE SUR. DUNFERMLINE

VEYOR EDIN.

May Island

Light Ho.

GERMAN

I stayed just a month as a warden – a month of sunsets and sunrises, of painting walkways, clearing beaches, digging out wells, clearing turf from paths, scrubbing steps and algae-ridden landings, building bird hides. The keepers' cottages overlooked some medieval ruins, and I pored over archaeological reports and paced out the distances to pre-Christian burial grounds. In a 900-year-old chapterhouse I hunkered down next to eider ducks on their nests.

At the north and south ends of the island there were abandoned foghorn towers, whitewashed and three storeys high. At the top of one of these towers of silence I found the corpse of an Arctic tern. There was a ring around one of its legs; with the help of one of the ornithologists we looked up its code. The ring testified that the tern had travelled the length of the Atlantic, Arctic to Antarctic, as often as I.

There were three lighthouses on the island. The oldest was the beacon Alexander Selkirk would have known, truncated and ruined at the suggestion of Sir Walter Scott, then crenellated by the Victorians. The 'Low Light' on the east shore had long been disused, and was given over to visiting ornithologists – this was the lighthouse where Keith Brockie had stayed for the year of painting and sketching that became *One Man's Island*. The largest lighthouse, crowning the island's summit, was separate from the lighthouse keepers' cottages, and was built, like so many around Scotland's coasts, by the Stevenson family. It was automated when I visited, but the principal warden held a key: she and I picked our way through its Victorian rooms. Their marble fireplaces were dusty and cold, their floorboards cracked and rotten.

On the rocks of the southeastern beaches of the May it was possible to explore the twisted iron remains of a ship wrecked in 1937, the *Island*, a Danish vessel that had made almost three hundred runs between Denmark, Iceland and Leith before losing its way in fog. Sixty-six were on board and all survived, the ship being beached high up on the strand line. Five days after the wrecking, the inhabitants of the newly established bird observatory boarded the vessel and took off any food, crockery and bedding they could carry. *The daily log entries from that year describe these events vividly*, wrote Brockie, *and crockery with the Danish Seaways imprint is still in use in the Low Light.*

The island has claimed the *Island*; its twisted plates of steel have been pushed higher up the beach by decades of successive storms, a memento mori for mariners, and a cautionary reminder of the power of the sea.

In a book about the Isle of May by W.J. Eggeling I read that Sir Walter Scott, on visiting the island, declared that it would make a *delightful residence for sea bathers*. But the appropriately named ornithologist W. Eagle Clarke lobbied for it to become a bird reserve instead. The log of the bird observatory suggests both of them had their way:

September 1st, 1947. A white form was seen on the rocks which on closer examination proved to be a naked woman. We thought it advisable to move on.

The party is agreed that should any more naked ladies be observed . . . they should be ringed to discover if the same individuals visit the island year after year.

More than a decade after my spell as a warden, by then a father and an ostensibly settled professional, I revisited the Isle of May. It was early summer, and I sailed on the tourist boat from Fife. No albatross trailed the ship, but a pod of dolphins like steel blades sliced straight for the hull and then veered away; puffins paddled out of our way. Ashore, nesting terns rose in a cloud from the ruined chapel, cormorants squared up to the waves like prize-fighters entering the ring. My children ran off from the jetty to play, their faces flushed with the thrill of summer's growth and change. And sunlight glittered over the ocean, diamonds on blue silk, sky and sea embracing along every horizon. A distant music sang through my mind, a dreamlike poem of Auden who knew the gifts of connection and of isolation. The poem, 'Seascape', speaks of delight in leaping island light, of shingle scrambling along whispering lines of surf, and compares the way clouds glide over the mirror of the sea to the movement of images through memory. It begins hypnotically: *Look, stranger, on this island now . . .*

I walked up to the main lighthouse, now open to the public and all cleaned up. The dusty rooms I'd once picked my way through were scrubbed and newly painted, and an exhibition of island artwork hung on the walls. The lantern of the light itself had been converted to solar power; instead of burning fossil fuels, sunlight was now caught by an array of solar panels, cradled in battery packs, then flashed out overnight *In Salutem Omnium.*

Islands and seabirds, seabirds and islands – the sound of gulls a shorthand for home.

TREASURE ISLANDS

THE DECISION TO live and work at Halley Research Station in Antarctica was perhaps the most extreme manifestation of my isle-o-philia. The obsession that pulled me to Iona, to the Andamans, to Tierra del Fuego as well as to the Isle of May, drew me to the most remote research station operated by the British government, isolated for ten months of the year, and about a thousand kilometres from its nearest neighbour. During my year there I read up on the scientific literature of what are known to aerospace psychologists as 'isolated and confined environments' – a category usually taken to mean oil rigs and polar bases, and which once included lighthouse keepers and deep-sea sailors. These environments are studied for the analogies they offer with deployment to space stations, and to prepare for an eventual mission to Mars.

One paper, in the *International Review of Applied Psychology*, found that Antarctic overwinterers became easier to hypnotise after a year of isolation, and their brainwaves changed shape. They also concluded that polar isolation induced *already self-sufficient, controlled, calm men to become even more so.*

This paper was published in the 1970s. It was thirty years before the body of research on isolated and confined environments began to show that women cope better than men with the pressures of Antarctic living, but were less likely to be selected at interview.

A journalist who met Alexander Selkirk in London after his long isolation commented: *He had a strong but chearful Seriousness in his Look, and a certain Disregard to the ordinary things about him, as if he had been sunk in Thought.*

I am uncertain if I became easier to hypnotise after my fourteen-month stay in Antarctica, but don't doubt my brainwaves altered. Another gift of the place was a recurring dream that began there, but continued for many months after my return. I'd be out skiing, far from base, a tiny figure moving between a vast plain of ice and a still vaster sky, when a crack began to open in the ice ahead of me. The base was constructed on a shelf of floating continental ice, easing itself out over the Weddell Sea, and so beneath my feet I knew there were hundreds of metres of polar seawater close to the point of freezing.

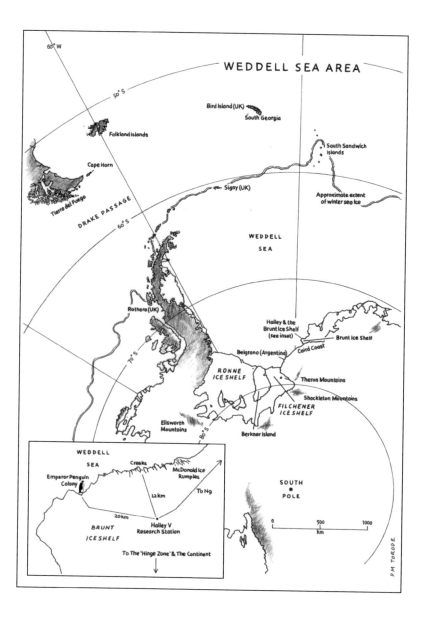

WEDDELL SEA AREA

60° W

50° S

Bird Island (UK)
South Georgia

Falkland Islands

South Sandwich Islands

Cape Horn

Signy (UK)

Approximate extent of winter sea Ice

Tierra del Fuego

DRAKE PASSAGE

60° S

WEDDELL SEA

Rothera (UK)

70° S

Halley & the Brunt Ice Shelf (see inset)

Brunt Ice Shelf

Caird Coast

Belgrano (Argentina)

RONNE ICE SHELF

Theron Mountains

Shackleton Mountains

FILCHENER ICE SHELF

Ellsworth Mountains

80° S

Berkner Island

SOUTH POLE

WEDDELL SEA

Creeks

McDonald Ice Rumples

Emperor Penguin Colony

12 km

To N9

20 km

Halley V Research Station

BRUNT ICE SHELF

0   500   1000
km

To The 'Hinge Zone' & The Continent

P. M. TOROPE

As the chasm in the ice advanced I'd race towards the base, straining every muscle to leap the crack before becoming marooned. I'd always wake at the same moment, airborne over the widening gulf, not knowing if I'd reconnect with the ice.

Of his journey to Iceland, William Morris wrote:

sometimes I like the idea of it, and sometimes it fills me with dismay.

Crusoe's terror on becoming separated from his island prison:

And now I began to give myself over for lost; for as the current was on both sides of the island, I knew in a few leagues' distance they must join again, and then I was irrecoverably gone . . .

And now I saw how easy it was for the Providence of God to make the most miserable condition mankind could be in, worse. Now I looked back upon my desolate solitary island as the most pleasant place in the world.

DANIEL DEFOE

Not long after my departure from Halley it became connected by satellite to the internet. But my dream has, in a sense, come true: an evolving crack in the ice shelf, accelerated by climate change, now risks calving the whole base adrift into the ocean. As a consequence, the research station has been abandoned for winter use.

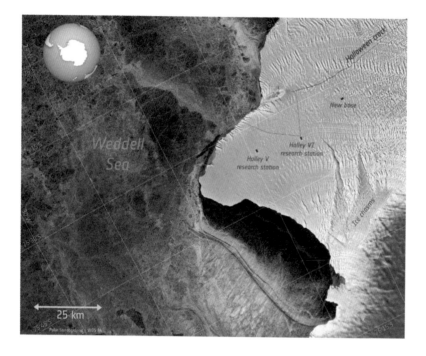

From his shipwreck, Crusoe recovered a pile of gold and silver coins, and Defoe recounts his internal monologue: *What art thou good for? . . . I have no manner of use for thee.* But then, *upon second thoughts, I took it away, and wrapping all this in a piece of canvas, I began to think of making another raft.*

Perhaps all islands offer the promise of treasure, of one kind or another. I now see that the book I wrote about Halley, *Empire Antarctica*, was a series of soundings for treasure, made into landscape composed solely of ice and of light.

Treasure Island

After three years on Treasure Island Ben Gunn degenerates, beast-like, something that also happened to the real-life sixteenth-century Spaniard Pedro Serrano who, marooned for seven years on an island in the Pacific, was eventually rescued but whose saviours found him irretrievably mad.

For Jim Hawkins the gold lies *thick as autumn leaves* but as long as he stays on the island its riches are worthless to him. Question: do the riches of island-living only make themselves manifest once you're back on the mainland?

Daniel Defoe didn't expect *Robinson Crusoe* to be such a success on publication: in that year alone, 1719, he published sixteen other pieces of writing. His sequels never found the same readership – it turned out readers were less interested in Crusoe's further adventures at sea, or in the Far East, than they were in the singular fact of his being marooned.

Elephant Island

In 1914 the polar explorer Ernest Shackleton set out to traverse Antarctica, but before reaching it his ship, the *Endurance*, was crushed by the vice-like winter ice of the Weddell Sea. Shackleton resolved with his crew to drag lifeboats hundreds of miles across jagged ice fields towards open water. After great privation they reached Elephant Island, off the Antarctic Peninsula.

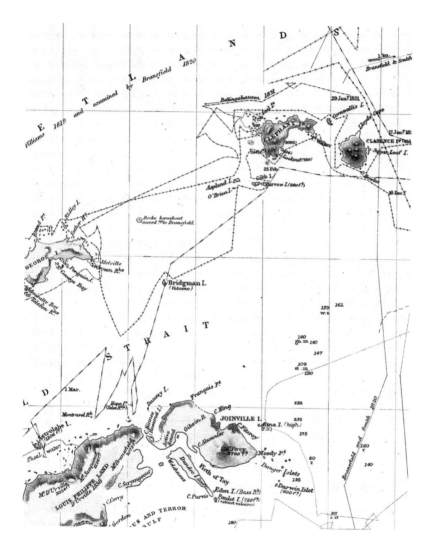

At the outset of this journey Shackleton is said to have stood in view of his men and carefully turned out his pockets of money, letting it fall to the ice. On the journey they were about to take, he said, they didn't need such trash weighing them down. Also in his pocket was a volume of the poems of Robert Browning, but he baulked at throwing it away.

Haply some philanthropic god steers bark,
Gift-laden, to the lonely ignorance
Islanded, say, where mist and snow mass hard

ROBERT BROWNING

Juan Fernandez
Alexander Selkirk was eager to make his fortune early – records from his village in Fife report that in 1693, at the age of seventeen, he was called to the Kirk Session to answer charges of indecent conduct, but did not appear *being gone to sea*. He became a privateer with the notorious William Dampier, as navigator on a second ship skippered by one Captain Stradling. By September 1704 he was insisting to Stradling and the rest of the crew that the ship was unseaworthy. He had been hoping to start a mutiny and force a refit of the ship, but instead Stradling marooned him with *clothes and bedding, a pistol, gunpowder, bullets, a hatchet, a knife, a pot in which to boil food, a bible, a book of prayers, his navigation instruments, and charts on how to read the imprisoning sea.*

This turned out to be all he needed. And he was right: Stradling's ship went on to founder, and those of his former crewmates who survived were enslaved by the Spanish.

Selkirk's isolation lasted just four years and four months, not the twenty-eight years, two months and nineteen days of Crusoe's fictional confinement – comparable rather to Nelson Mandela's incarceration, the majority of which was on Robben Island.

Robben Island

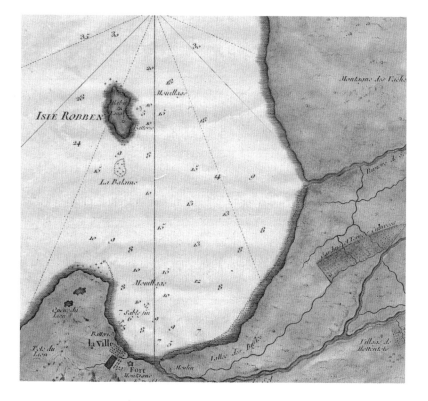

In May 1720, a few years after Selkirk's rescue and a year after the publication of *Robinson Crusoe*, another British pirate, George Shelvocke, was shipwrecked on Juan Fernandez with some of his crew. Over the following five months Shelvocke built an escape vessel from the wreckage. Again, several of the crew were convinced the escape vessel was unseaworthy, and there seems to have been a mutiny: *Eleven or twelve renegades, with a similar number of Blacks and Indians, had deserted the main party while on the island, and refused to leave with the rest.*

These 'renegades' were picked up two years later by the Spanish, and enslaved.

Shelvocke's book – *A Voyage Round the World by Way of the Great South Sea* – like Defoe's, was widely read. William Wordsworth and Samuel Taylor Coleridge treasured it, and parts of Shelvocke's story were transferred wholesale into Coleridge's *The Rime of the Ancient Mariner.*

We had not had the sight of one fish of any kind since we were come to the Southward of the Straits of Le Maire; nor one sea-bird excepting a disconsolate black albatross, who accompanied us for several days, hovering about us as if he had lost himself.

GEORGE SHELVOCKE

Shelvocke's mate Hatley decided that the bird was an ill omen and, in a *melancholy fit*, shot it – an act Shelvocke deplored.

I never saw the albatross in Unst – by the time of my visit it had moved on to another rocky outcrop closer to the Hebrides, called Sula Sgeir.

For an albatross, this was like moving just a few doors down the same street.

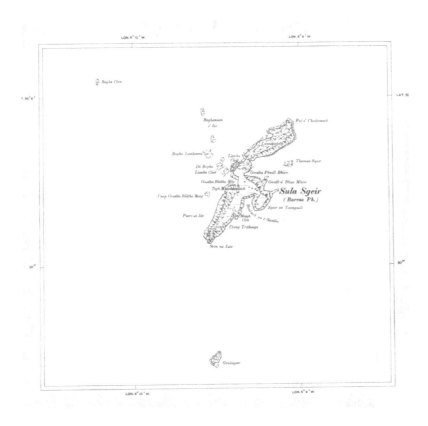

TOWARDS RESOLUTION

THERE ARE TIMES in the city when I have to remind myself that *connectedness* too has its appeal: urban living offers limitless opportunities for engagement, as does travel, with what Montaigne called its capacity to *rub and polish our brain* with the ideas of others.

In the Andaman Islands, resting each day in the shade of palm trees in the company of the remorseful, war-traumatised Israeli couple, it became apparent to me that isolation and connection were the two energising poles of my life. First, immersion in medical practice for its intensity, its social engagement, its ringside seat to all the bustle and brilliance of humanity. And then island postings and polar travel – for the distance and perspective they grant, for the chance to feel part of a world somewhat emptied of the human, for their silence and space for contemplation.

Were a vantage point ever achievable my track between these two poles could be seen as a sinusoidal wave swerving relentlessly from one to the other.

On an Orkney ferry once I met a woman born on a small island in Malaysia, trained as an engineer, who had been transplanted to Scotland by the might and reach of the international petrochemical industry. I asked her why even here, on the other side of the planet from her home, she was drawn to visiting islands. *There's only so much as a visitor you can do here*, she said of Orkney. *For the first few days I was cycling and thinking about home and work and worries, but then that just settled and there was nothing left but emptiness. For me the gift of this place is emptiness.*

Is it, then, that for visitors outside the community for whom the island is home, the gift of an island is its *curtailment* of opportunity? That they offer time to journey *in*, rather than opportunities for attention to be directed *out*?

Donald Winnicott believed that periods of emptiness and silence, renouncing new experience, were profoundly help-ful for the psyche. That if we become sufficiently isolated, but at the same time protected from negative influences, our minds find ways to heal themselves.

If we can adjust ourselves to these natural processes, we can leave most of these complex mechanisms [of recovery] to nature, while we sit back and watch and learn.

. . . As a psychoanalyst I have had very good training in this matter of waiting and waiting and waiting.

DONALD WINNICOTT

For outsiders, islands offer many opportunities for waiting, for patience, perhaps for the kind of healing Winnicott had in mind.

After fifteen years of going back and forward between isolation and connection I tried combining the two, and looked for sustaining, collaborative, engaging work on islands – work I was lucky enough to find. But just as it's in the nature of the north and south poles that they can never be brought together, in the longer term, these twinned enthusiasms of my life were to resist being combined.

The Scots poet Hugh MacDiarmid believed that it was a mark of distinction to be able to hold two opposing points of view simultaneously.

Do I contradict myself?
Very well then I contradict myself

WALT WHITMAN

The gift of this place is emptiness, the Malaysian engineer said of Orkney. But for a doctor, working life is always full – of interactions, of experience, of talk, of thought, of demands.

On the Isle of Skye I once conducted GP clinics in the village of Uig, its bay yawning with nonchalance at the Outer Hebrides and the grey gods of the Atlantic. I also conducted a clinic on the island of Raasay, on the eastern side of Skye. The district nurse met me at the pier and drove me on a tour of her island, to visit the few housebound patients who needed medical attention. As a doctor, attending to the people for whom the island is home, there was little time for contemplation.

My survey of Raasay did not furnish much which can interest my readers, wrote James Boswell of his journey around the Hebrides with Samuel Johnson. *I shall therefore put it into as short a compass as I can.*

Zamalek   Before leaving for Antarctica I'd fallen in love with E., a woman who shared my isle-o-philia, but who was also drawn to places noted for the vibrant intensity of their human connections. One of our first adventures together began on a boat on the Nile, moored beside the river-island of Zamalek.

As I sailed towards the South Pole she took a job in Beirut; a year and a half later we were reunited. Together, we began to broker a reconciliation between these two conflicting passions.

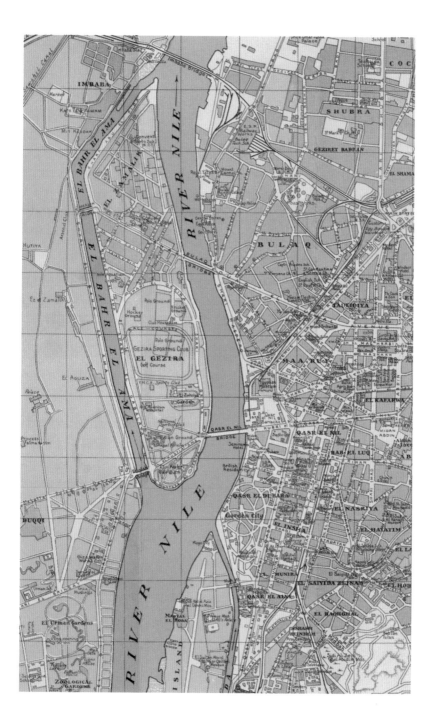

I've described my first journey to Orkney at midwinter, shortly before departing for Athos. My second was a camping trip in midsummer, with E., by foot ferry from John o'Groats, across a firth Defoe in his *A Tour Thro' the Whole Island of Great Britain* (1724–27) described as being haunted by witches.

    'Tis spoken much of as dangerous for ships, he said.

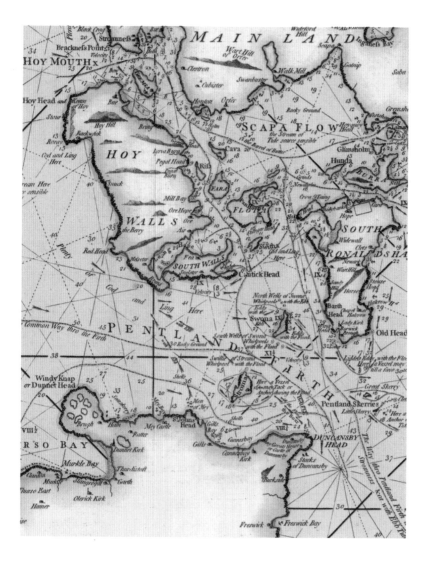

The first twenty-two chapter titles of *Robinson Crusoe* begin with an 'I': *I Am Captured by Pirates / I Sow My Grain / I See the Shore Spread with Bones*. Then Crusoe meets Friday, and there come five chapter titles that begin 'We': *We Make Another Canoe / We Plan a Voyage / We Seize the Ship*. The reader understands that only as a couple is there hope of ever leaving the island.

At the tidal island of Birsay off the northwestern coast of
Orkney's Mainland, E. and I wandered the ruins of a
medieval Norse village, built for defence. Puffins and
fulmars inhabit it now. The warden was a Canadian isle-
o-philiac magician recently arrived from Japan by way of
Warsaw. It was his ambition to perform a magic trick on
every inhabited island in Scotland. He had reached forty-
five, about halfway through his list.

We moved onwards to the island of Egilsay, with its fields of camomile. In Wyre we stumbled over another Norse fortress crumbled to stone hurdles, and paid homage to the poet Edwin Muir who grew up there. Of his childhood in Wyre, and his rude awakening from an idyllic island life into a difficult, orphaned adolescence in Glasgow, Muir wrote:

I was born before the Industrial Revolution and am now about two hundred years old . . . in 1751 I set out from Orkney for Glasgow. When I arrived I found that it was not 1751, but 1901.

EDWIN MUIR

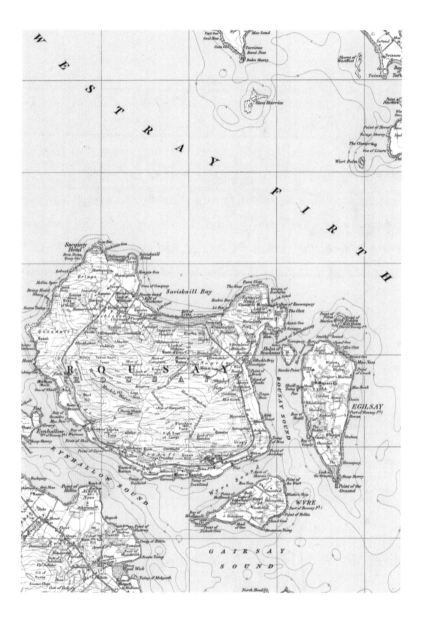

On the island of Rousay there were interpretation boards about the Traill family: unjust Victorian lairds, imperial military adventurers, emigrants. Among the family's many destinations was New Zealand. In 1900 one of the furthest travelled of the Traills, Charles, finished up in Stewart Island/Rakiura, at the opposite extremity of the British imperial world, after trying his luck in the Californian gold fields and in Australia. He must have been another isle-o-phile, having travelled the span of the globe to make his home on another island, off an island, off a continent.

His half-brother Walter, who grew up on the Fife coast, retired to join him there after a life at sea catching seals. Another Orkney islander, Arthur Traill, was the local schoolteacher and Justice of the Peace.

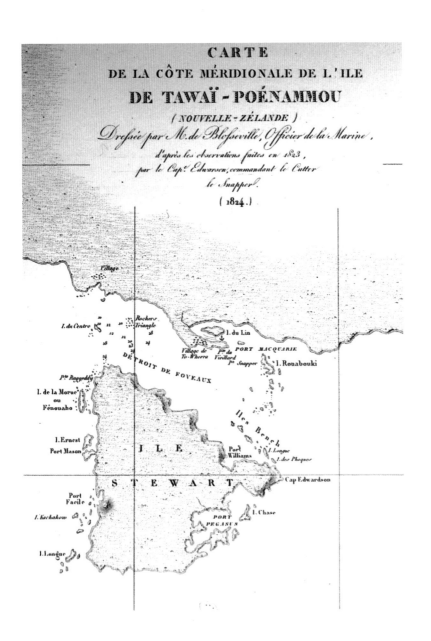

CARTE
DE LA CÔTE MÉRIDIONALE DE L'ILE
DE TAWAÏ - POÉNAMMOU
(NOUVELLE - ZÉLANDE)

Dressée par M. de Blosseville, Officier de la Marine,

d'après les observations faites en 1823,

par le Cap.ⁿᵉ Edwarsen, commandant le Cutter

le Snapper.

(1824.)

Village

I. du Centre

Rochers Triangle

I. du Lin

Village de To-Wheera

P.ᵗᵉ de Vieillard

PORT MACQUARIE

P.ᵗᵉ Snapper

I. Rouabouki

DÉTROIT DE FOVEAUX

P.ᵗᵉ Raggedty

I. de la Morue ou Fénouaho

Iles Bench

I. Ernest

Port Mason

I L E

Port Williams

I. Longue

I. des Phoques

S T E W A R T

Cap Edwardson

Port Facile

I. Kachahow

PORT PEGASUS

I. Chase

I. Longue

Some years later E. and I made it together to Stewart Island, following an eighteen-month journey, by motorcycle, that began in Orkney. The resonances in the landscape between the northern and southern extremities of our journey were profound. As we sailed south from the ferry port of Bluff, albatrosses swooped over the waves around the ferry. There was a park there named for the Traills, in the settlement called Oban.

Like that albatross in Unst, it felt as if the Traills were in search not just of an island to call home, but an island climate brutal enough for their comfort; the names of the settlements reflected not only Orcadian influence, but that of Shetlanders. Shortly after reaching Stewart Island, we returned to Europe.

Orkney

E. and I camped our way across ten or twelve of the Orkney Islands, and a year or so later, as she finished some studies, I took a job on one of them. As part of this job I conducted clinics in North Ronaldsay, where I'd gone five years earlier as a winter prelude to the isolation of Athos.

The sound of waves crashing on the shingle penetrated to the centre of the island – I was reminded of the Pacific roar Darwin described as being audible on the east side of Chiloé. There were few patients; E. had stayed in Kirkwall in Orkney's Mainland; I walked circuits of the beach. Again I found myself watching sunsets with seals curled at my feet, snoozing and jerking in restless seal-dreams. Fulmars flew within inches of my feet – with no cliffs to play off, they glided along the strand line instead.

Fast-forward three or four years, and we returned to living and working in Orkney, this time in the town of Stromness, along a curl of coast in the west of the Mainland. We had become parents; our baby was just three months old. Every Friday afternoon I'd take the ferry out to Flotta, one of the smaller islands south of Scapa Flow, where an old car, its key in the ignition, waited on the pier for my arrival. I'd drive it up to the medical clinic, which doubled as home to the island's resident nurse. *Flotta*

At that time two nurses worked the island in shifts: Valerie and Elaine. Valerie so enjoyed Orkney that she rented a cottage on its Mainland to use whenever she was off duty. Elaine was from London, and flew back there whenever she had leave.

After I'd seen a few patients, and talked over any difficulties, we'd go together to watch seabirds along the crests of the cliffs. Elaine would talk about Zimbabwe, where she grew up, and how she used her spare time on the island to write a novel she'd been planning for years, a novel that touched on the devastation of war that transformed Rhodesia into Zimbabwe.

From Flotta, the coastline of Scotland was just visible along the southern horizon; to the west was Hoy, 'high island' to *Hoy* the Norse, whose hills were once topped with beacons to alert the people of Orkney to approaching pirates.

But the love of the rock and of the mountain still wrought on Erland's mind, and he fixed his dwelling not on the soft hills of Orphir, or the green plains of Graemsay, but in the wild and mountainous Isle of Hoy, whose summit rises to the sky like the cliffs of Foula and of Faroe.

SIR WALTER SCOTT

Sir Walter Scott travelled among the Orkney Islands in 1814, the same year he visited the Isle of May, and in a footnote to *The Pirate* records this anecdote of its birdlife: *An individual was living in Orkney not long since, whom, while a child in its swaddling clothes, an eagle actually transported to its nest in the hill of Hoy. Happily the eyry being known, and the bird instantly pursued, the child was found uninjured, playing with the young eagles.*

I heard the same story in the Faroese island of Vágar, from where an eagle is said to have abducted a baby and flown it to its nest on the jagged pinnacles of Tindhólmur Island. But in that harsher, colder, more blasted archipelago, the story didn't end so well for the child.

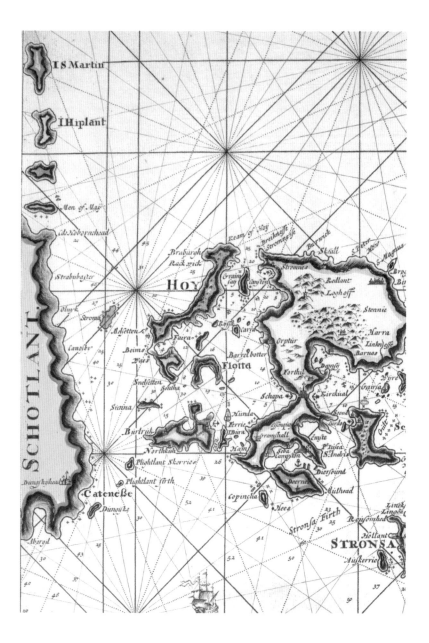

I S Martin

I Hiplant

Men of Mai

Ce. Nobor…head

Strabubaiter

Oluyk

Stroma

Brabargh
Rack.wick

Ream of Hoy
Breikneffe
Stromnes ist

Burwick
Skeall
S. Petr
Magnus
Broo
Bir

HOY

Grain
bay
Canyton

Stromnes

Redlant
Logh off

Stennie

M. Sötten

Faira

Elwis
Carja

Orptur

Marra
Linkneffe
Barnas

SCHOTLANT

Canofer

Beims
Wair

Barrelbotter

Floita

Forthil

Danzö

Snelfelten
Seluha

Sunna

Burlruh

Schapa

Kirkwal
Gairja
Se

Northkuh

Munda
Perrie
Buri

Elfongion
Gramfhall

Ham

Seba
Canyton

Emite
P. tifea
S. Inelcia

Plightlant Skerries

Sond
Gurdo
Grott

Dungihead

Plightlant Firth

Copincha

Dierfound
Muthead

Deerne

C ateneße

Dungike

Hee

Stronfa Firth

Reufomhed

Linek
Lingom

Abergd

STRONSA

Hottant

Aufkerrie

ISLAND DREAMS

IN A SECOND-HAND bookshop in Orkney I found a copy of *Laterna Magica* by the Faroese writer William Heinesen. Of the drama of island life he wrote: *Ah yes, nothing much happens in a little, stagnant town at the end of the world, practically nothing measured by the yardstick of the worldly man. And yet a lot does happen, quite honestly much more than even the inquisitive soul, eager to learn, can manage to absorb.*

Orkney has, and has had, many poets, some of them far-travelled. Edwin Muir may have grown up on the island of Wyre, but after Glasgow he moved to London, Edinburgh, Prague, Rome and Cambridge, Massachusetts, among other places.

By contrast his pupil, George Mackay Brown, stayed in Orkney, concerned less with the costs of island living than with its rewards. He made brief journeys south, rarely further than Edinburgh. For him, to be an islander offered community and a social ecology that was healthier for being simpler, more *comprehensible*.

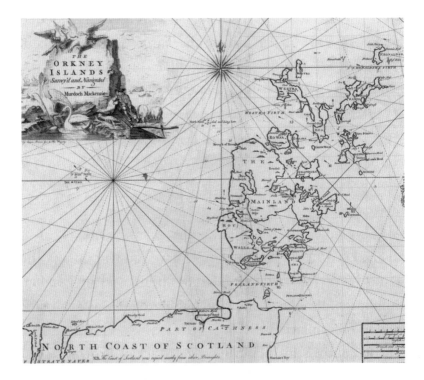

In the story 'The Silent Guests', Heinesen tells a tale of two sons of the Faroes who grew up to become poets. One was a lawyer and sailed far abroad, living a life which was rich in drama and excitement, *but he was homeless and unlucky in love . . . he sang of the Sirens and the Furies and the incurable wounds of storm-tossed hearts.* The other brother stayed in the Faroe Islands with his mother and wife, *and sang of happily playing children and the slumbering ducks on the sandy shore by the mouth of the river under the twinkling of familiar stars.*

The island: a whole world where all the intricacies and complexities of human life are reproduced in miniature? Or a cloister, split off from the world, from industry, from the decisive action of history?

Just take the kids to the beach, said a friend, *and that way they entertain themselves.* Are these dreams of islands simply an echo of childhood happiness?

When Alexander Selkirk was rescued, the captain of the relieving ship, Woodes Rogers, wrote: *Our Pinnace return'd from the shore and brought abundance of Craw-Fish with a Man cloth'd in Goat Skins who look'd wilder than the first Owners of them.*

This was not the first ship to visit the island since Selkirk had been marooned – a couple of years earlier a crew of Spaniards had put in, recognised the sole inhabitant as British, and hunted him with dogs. He'd run into the forests and scaled a tree. One of the Spaniards tracked him to the base of it; Selkirk looked down, terrified, holding his breath until the Spaniard gave up the chase. If he had been caught he would have been killed, or transferred to slavery in the Bolivian silver mines.

When, two years later, Selkirk realised that the ship approaching his shores was of Englishmen he rushed down to the beach to greet them. The sailors stared at him dumbfounded as he attempted to speak. His throat was tight, his mouth dry, and he struggled even to stutter *ma-rooned . . . ma-rooned . . .*

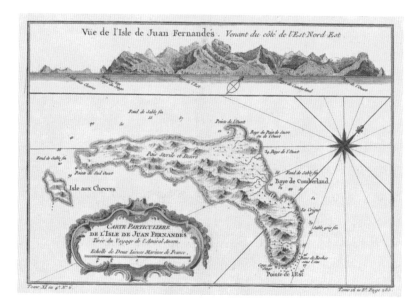

*He had so much forgot his Language for want of Use
that we could scarce understand him, for he seemed to
speak his words by halves.*

WOODES ROGERS

When we chose, as a family, to live on an island, and for
me to take work there as a doctor, I did nothing but talk.
It's the job of a physician after all – to talk, to empathise,
sympathise, comprehend. There are a few branches of
medicine that can be conducted silently, but most doctors
use words all day long, trying to tease out a mental map
of another human being's experience and explain their
way, through words, towards release from distress.

I have an abiding love of Orkney. But I soon began
to feel that its Mainland was too dense with connections;
in order to feel what might amount to a sense of isolation I'd have to strike out for occasional trips to even
smaller islands. This is how I came to frequent the island
of Hoy.

In the village of Rackwick, in Hoy, a few cottages serve
now for the most part as second homes, hunkered down in
a great amphitheatre of a valley that gapes towards the
northern coast of Scotland. By the beach was a stone bothy
where I'd often be the only visitor. One sunset evening I
heard the skirl of bagpipes – I emerged from the bothy to
see a man standing out on the shingle, playing to a bobbing
audience of seals.

Hoy

On another visit to Rackwick I arrived at the beach to find five kids there, late teens, who'd driven from the south end of the island *for the crack*. They handed me one of their beers from a cardboard case. They told me that there were no police officers on the island, but that as Hoy folk born and raised, they'd never abuse their liberation from the law. *Stromness folk come over and tear up and down drunk in their cars*, one of teenagers said, shaking his head in disbelief. *Those folk from the Mainland, they jist don't know how to behave.*

This regression to ever-smaller islands is the sequence described by D.H. Lawrence in 'The Man Who Loved Islands', a peculiar story of a wealthy man who purchases, then lives on, a series of islands. As patterns of connections and relationships becomes established in each he begins to think of it with rancour, so abandons it for one smaller, more remote, more *isolated*.

Lawrence was both attracted and repulsed by the notion of island isolation. He begins one book, *Sea and Sardinia*, with the words *Comes over one an absolute necessity to move*, then goes on to describe how in 1921 he abandoned one admittedly large island, Sicily, for another, Sardinia. *Strange how this coast-country does not belong to our present-day world*, he wrote of the islands along the north-east of the Sardinian coast. *Still this coast-country was forsaken, forgotten, not included. It just is not included.*

Is it necessary for the cartographer to spend long in a place in order to map it? It could be argued that brevity of experience encourages the kind of distilled perspective required for effective cartography. These days cartographers rarely pace out the lines of the maps they draw. Melville spent just four weeks in the Marquesa Islands researching *Typee*, less time than I've spent on the Isle of May. Yet his book about the experience was the most widely read of his lifetime.

The protagonist of Lawrence's 'The Man Who Loved Islands' finds himself at last on a small Atlantic island, *just a few acres of rock*. It has some turf, some rainwater, rocks, sedge and seabirds. He has abandoned his naïve new wife and newborn daughter to move there. And on this island his solitude becomes a mania: he eyes passing steamers with distrust, fearful they'll attempt to communicate with him, while sinking into a stupor of isolation. Lawrence describes a wandering, spectral figure, surrounded by luminous fogs, *absolutely alone, with the space soaking into him. The grey sea alone, and the footing of his sea-washed island*.

There's an unwholesome puritanism about Lawrence's island lover, the rich man seeking his protected domain with the kind of obsessive intolerance that turns loyalty to bigotry, love into hate. His love of islands leads him to abandon family and friends, to seek doom and oblivion.

At the end he dies muttering: *The elements! The elements!*

'We feel we're not doing right by the children,' said those who had children. 'We feel we're not doing right by ourselves,' said those who had no children. And the various families fairly came to hate one another.

   Yet the island was so lovely . . .

D.H. LAWRENCE

In the end Lawrence wasn't much of an isle-o-phile. *I don't care for islands*, he wrote from the French Îles d'Hyères, *especially very small ones*.

Îles d'Hyères

In Peter Matthiessen's *The Snow Leopard*, the author records his conversation with a Buddhist lama high in the Himalayas. *Of course I am happy here!* said the lama. *It's wonderful! Especially because I have no choice!*

Matthiessen's wife had died not long before his departure. He was grieving, and felt guilty: in order to reach the high isolation of the Himalayas he had left his eight-year-old son, who had just lost a mother, at home in America.

There were nights in Orkney when I'd be up changing a nappy, or comforting the baby, when Matthiessen's description not of the Himalayas, but of Antarctica, resounded in my mind. *Its excruciating purity and vast healing silence ring with creation*, he wrote, *ancient and yet new, and fresh beyond imagining.* It was a comfort to know that it was still there.

Alexander Selkirk returned to Britain a wealthy man, rich on plunder taken with his rescuers on the long voyage home. He returned briefly to Fife, then eloped to London with a young dairymaid called Sophia Bruce. Settled life apparently didn't suit him – within three years he turned up in Plymouth, as master's mate on a pirate-hunting ship bound for the Gold Coast, the HMS *Weymouth*.

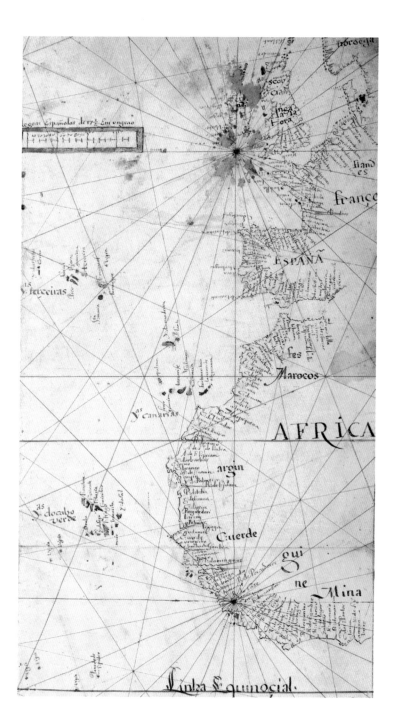

legoas Espanolas de 17½ Em onquao

norscga

scor
cia

Ingla
tora

fland
es

france

ESPAÑA

y terceiras

fes

Marocos

Y canarias

AFRICA

argin

as docabo
verde

Cuerde

gui

ne

Mina

Linha Equinoçial.

A few days before the *Weymouth* sailed he got married again, this time to an innkeeper called Frances Candis. A few months into his African voyage, sailing down the Guinea coast, he died, likely of yellow fever, and was buried at sea. He was forty-five. His two widows engaged lawyers to fight over his estate. Frances won; Sophia was thrown in a debtors' prison.

In the library I come across a book called *Dream Islands*. It is large and glossy, all palm trees and beaches, any hint of refuse or the effluent of human settlement airbrushed away. The enduring popularity of *Robinson Crusoe* rests on just such a dream, but also on the human instinct to wonder of any extreme or unusual experience, *if it was me, how would I cope?*

When I returned from Antarctica this was the real demand behind the recurring question, *so, tell me, what was it like?*

Selkirk abandoned one wife, then another, for his love affair with the sea. Lawrence's protagonist dies delirious and alone for the purity of his dream. But I'm sure the poles of isolation and connection aren't as irreconcilable as these two stories suggest – there may well be more creative ways of bringing them together.

There's a Hindu tradition that divides life into four phases: a youthful phase focused on learning and exploration (*brahmacharya*), followed by a householder phase focused on family and profession (*grihastha*). This second phase seems to involve giving up a measure of independence in order to forge connections that yield more than the sum of their parts.

If reconciliation between the poles of isolation and connection is possible, perhaps it's only in the subsequent phase of retreat (*vanaprastha*), or the final phase of renunciation (*sannyasa*). In those phases, ties to work and family loosen. But for the Hindu ascetic, connections to the people around you are loosened for the purpose of feeling more connected to *everything*.

A dream I wrote down during that time in Orkney, when E. and I were finding our feet as parents, and as members of the island community. In the dream I was paddling a sinking inflatable dinghy through the waters of an antique map, the seas around me filled with otherworldly creatures of the deep.

I had two cases to keep dry: one a medical case, the other a kit for travelling. The dinghy sank further, the cases were getting wet. Frantic, I abandoned the dinghy, and the cases, then with a sense of liberation, swam to shore.

E. and I came to appreciate that being parents of a very young child had brought us to the threshold of a phase of life where isolation might have less to teach us than connection. We were building deeper links to our new island community, but at the same time older allegiances from our time in the city were already beginning to fade. If we were to have more children, keeping close to family and old friends would become more important than ever. At root this was a question of belonging: now, with children of our own, where was the place to which we most belonged? We resolved to return, for this chapter of parenthood at least, to the mainland.

The estuary we moved south to is a plexus of motion and connection. Aeroplanes bank above it to make their approach to Edinburgh Airport. There's a Victorian-era rail bridge, a colossal iron web of tubular struts and beams in red-painted steel. The colour of this bridge is part of its appeal – in the westering light of sunset it seems almost to swell, vivid and arterial against a deepening eastern sky. Tankers ease under its spans, kept off the sandbanks by tug boats. Every so often a floating hotel of a cruise ship moors mid-river by Inch Garvie, the uninhabited island that supports the bridge. And there's always the tide, the ceaseless tide. In Scotland the skies can be overcast for days – the motion of the water becomes the only evidence of the restless moon.

In the interlocking beams of the bridge there's something of the warp and weft of textiles. *Textile* and *text* share a root meaning *woven*, or *wrought*. Text too can be an interlocking network of supporting connections, a framework, a scaffold, a web. It can form a bridge into memory, a balm for isolation.

We have three children now. On an island holiday, at the age when their horizons began to extend beyond the family and out into the world, I asked them why they like visiting islands. *They have beaches all around,* said one; *they make you feel safe,* said another; *they have space to play and trees to climb,* said the third.

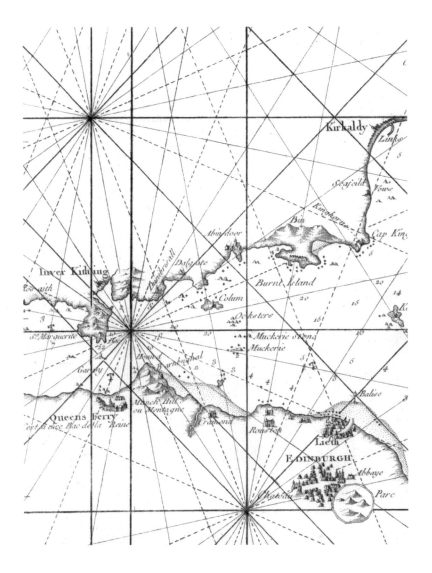

After four years on the shores of the estuary with our three young children, we moved again, from living near the water to the centre of the city in order to be closer to work. *Who are the neighbours?* the children asked, disorientated by a place where the streets were never quiet, where the ceaseless flow beyond the gate was no longer that of the tide, but a river of humanity. We introduced them to the neighbours, but the neighbours, too, flowed ceaselessly on.

The walls of the flat felt porous. Each evening, once the children were asleep, E. and I felt the city's plurality and potential to connect as an ambivalent force – warmly enveloping, but also threatening. In comparison with the insularity of the family it offered an immense continent of possibilities. Was the family, then, an island requiring protection?

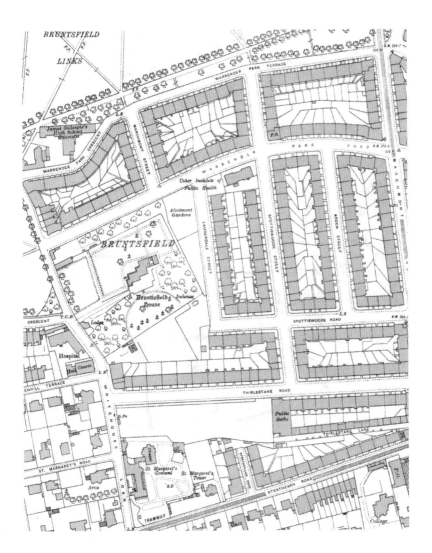

This may have been what Winnicott was getting at when he spoke of the need in psychological and emotional health for a measure of isolation.

Traditionally, going on pilgrimage has been one potential answer to this dilemma – the pilgrim cuts him or herself off from everything familiar in order to connect with countless anonymous others, past, future and present, on the road to Rome, or Varanasi, or Santiago de Compostela, or Lhasa, or Jerusalem – all places I've walked, amazed and islanded among surging, oceanic crowds of others.

A couple of decades ago fifty-eight skeletons were unearthed on the Isle of May during archaeological excavations. The youngest had been interred around five hundred years ago; the oldest a millennium before that, even as Brendan and Columba were making their island journeys from Ireland to Scotland's western coast.

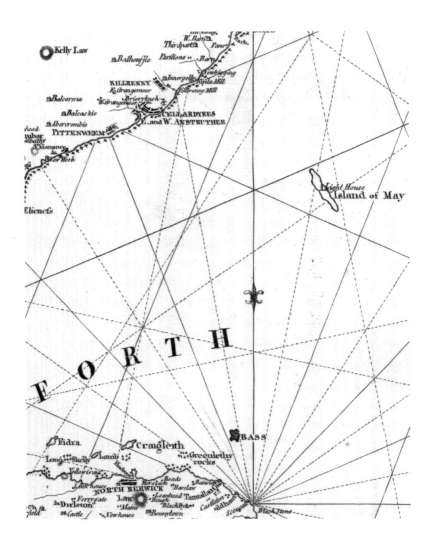

The skeletons were transferred to the storage facility of the National Museum of Scotland in South Queensferry where they lay for a few years. In 2016 Marlo Willows, a doctoral student in archaeology at the University of Edinburgh, published her investigation into the skeletons' unusually high rate of traumatic injuries – breaks in the bone that had subsequently healed. Among that ossuary was the earliest known case of prostate cancer, in someone whose bone composition suggested he'd grown up over a hundred miles away from the island. Also among the remains was the skeleton of an early medieval teenager, whose spine was contorted with congenital tuberculosis. *The severity of this individual's disease would have been crippling,* Willows noted, *indicating a parent or other family member accompanying them to the Isle of May for healing purposes.*

The remains were unearthed of a man who had grown up nearby. He was buried with a scallop shell, sometimes a signal for the hereafter that before dying the deceased had made the pilgrimage to Santiago de Compostela in Spain.

The Isle of May's medieval priory was likely a place of pilgrimage and of medicine; of retreat and peace after a life filled with connection. The monks there were obliged somehow to combine healing with that other life, of prayer without ceasing.

Prayer without ceasing is a good description of the quality of attention that Charles Darwin brought to the natural world. Wherever he looked he noticed subtleties that others had passed by. It was the isolation of the Galapagos Islands that gave Darwin the space and silence for his greatest revelations, but recounting them was something he did back home, surrounded by his books, family and art.

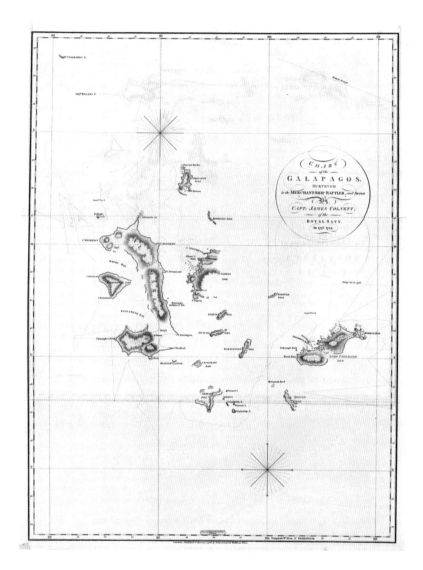

CHART
of the
GALAPAGOS,
SURVEYED
in the MERCHANT SHIP RATTLER, and drawn
by
CAPT. JAMES COLNETT,
of the
ROYAL NAVY,
in 1793 1794.

Darwin's final book on the habits of earthworms was published just a few months before his death at the age of seventy-three. As his thoughts turned to his own interment he watched the worms of his south London lawn with deepening interest. He'd been through a long phase of retreat, and entered one of renunciation. His book, when it appeared, was an instant bestseller, rivalling the sales of *On the Origin of Species.*

A monk on Mount Athos told me that he considered the monastic life a soft option, insisting that *he* had chosen the easy way to live, isolated from the distractions of society. *I've tried living the life I want surrounded by family, by friends, work*, he said, *but I just couldn't do it.*

Annie Dillard was less interested in the magical floating islands of Pliny than she was in real floating islands, mangroves, that she'd encountered in Florida and in the waters around the Galapagos Islands. *It walks teetering and wanton before the wind*, she wrote of the mangrove island. *What it is most likely to do is drift anywhere in the alien ocean, feeding on death and growing, netting a makeshift soil as it goes, shrimp in its toes and terns in its hair.*

Yet our planet too, she observed, is a floating island, *beautiful and loose*, bearing us across the great nowhere of space. Our planet, like the mangrove, generates its own soil as it goes, *rocking over the salt sea at random, rocking day and night and round the sun.*

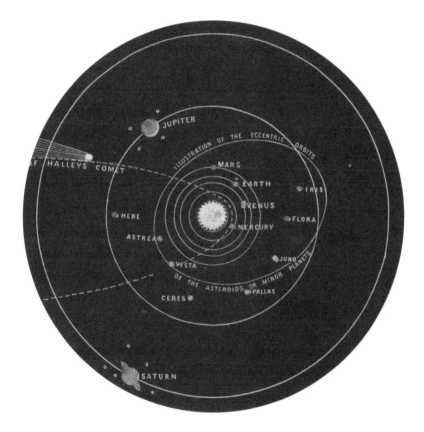

What is it I've been trying to capture? A sense of reverence, and an absence of distraction. Birds are essential to it, as emblems of motion, levity and transcendence. The familiar elements of sky and sea.

The goal might just be to carry your isolation with you, like Selkirk's measured calm as he met journalists in London, or Herman Melville's Queequeg, Pacific islander and harpoonist, who *never consorted at all, or but very little, with the other seamen in the inn . . . he seemed entirely at his ease; preserving the utmost serenity; content with his own companionship; always equal to himself.*

Sometimes it seems as if I'm no closer to solving the dilemma: push and pull, city and island, the torrent of life through the clinic, and its serenity lived in isolation.
But there's time.

We are all islanders.

THANKS

Stephen Grosz, Therese Alampo, Adam Nicolson, Keith Taylor, Eleanor Anderson, Ciaran Reid, Dominique le Fort, Claire Marlange, Josh Cohen, Jane Nash, Amanda Bragg, Mark Jensen, Annie Dillard, Paul Torode, Tom Kirby, Catherine Shepherd, Mark Newell, Charlie Siderfin, Andy Trevett, Valerie Holmes, Elaine Tsopotsa, Kathleen Jamie, Calum Morrison, Tam MacPhail, Mhairi Linklater, Jenny Brown, Paula Williams, Colin Thubron, Megan Reid, Francis Bickmore, Leila Cruickshank, Vicki Rutherford, Gill Heeley, Anna Frame, Seán Costello, Esa Aldegheri.

NOTES ON SOURCES

8 *However beautiful, with* . . . Rebecca Solnit, *A Field Guide to Getting Lost*. Edinburgh: Canongate, 2017.

8 *Images* (tu) *are the* . . . quoted in Jerry Brotton, *A History of the World in Twelve Maps*. London: Penguin, 2013.

10 *Reading the names* . . . Judith Schalansky, *Atlas of Remote Islands*. London: Particular Books, 2010.

10 *Inspire feelings of* . . . Thurston Clarke, *Islomania*. London: Abacus, 2002.

12 *The boy and girl at puberty* . . . Donald Winnicott, 'Communicating and Not Communicating'. In *The Collected Works of D.W. Winnicott*, Vol. 6. Oxford: Oxford University Press, 2016.

18 *The love of islands* . . . Adam Nicolson, *Sea Room*. London: HarperCollins, 2001.

20 *A stark tower* . . . Virginia Woolf, *To the Lighthouse*. London: Vintage, 2011.

26 *The island of* . . . *The Age of Bede*, ed. D.H. Farmer. London: Penguin, 1998.

26 *James, at six years old* . . . Helen Dunmore's introduction to Virginia Woolf, *To The Lighthouse*. London: Vintage, 2011.

26 *To dig, to bake* . . . Virginia Woolf, 'Robinson Crusoe' in *The Common Reader* Vol. II. London: Vintage, 2003.

28 *The ambushes of sex* . . . Louis MacNeice, *Letters from Iceland*. London: Faber, 1937.

28 *Was I not* . . . William Carlos Williams, 'The Practice'. In *The Doctor Stories*. New York: New Directions, 1984.

28 *First of all* . . . André Malraux (trans. Terence Kilmartin), *Anti-Memoirs*. London: Penguin, 1968.

29 *I will arise and* . . . from A. Norman Jeffares, *A New Commentary on the Poems of W.B. Yeats*. London: Pan Macmillan, 1984.

30 *Unfortunately many succumb* . . . Keith Brockie, *One Man's Island*. London: Dent, 1984.

32 *Islanders are always* . . . Joshua Slocum, *Sailing Alone Around the World*. London: Bloomsbury, 2015.

34 *I know pleasure still* . . . quoted in Claire Harman, *Robert Louis Stevenson: A Biography*. London HarperPerennial, 2012.

36 *A feeling of awe* . . . Slocum, *ibid.*

36 *Very low volume* . . . Sara Maitland, *A Book of Silence*. London: Granta, 2008.

40 *The sparsely inhabited* . . . John Berger, *Portraits*. London: Verso, 2016.

42 *There are costs* . . . Slocum, *ibid.*

42 *For Europe is absent* . . . W.H. Auden, *Letters from Iceland*. London: Faber, 1937.

43 *I, on my side* . . . Henry David Thoreau, *Walden*. London: Orion, 1995.

45 *With the Sandwich Islanders* . . . Charles Darwin, *The Expression of Emotion in Man and Animals*. Cambridge: Cambridge University Press, 2013.

45 *It was a lake* . . . Thoreau, *ibid.*

47 *The landscape's most beautiful* . . . Thoreau, *ibid.*

51 *A panorama more deplorably* . . . Edgar Allan Poe, 'A Descent into the Maelström' in *The Narrative of Arthur Gordon Pym of Nantucket and Related Tales*. Oxford: Oxford World Classics, 1994.

55 *I wander about* . . . Knut Hamsun (trans. Oliver and Gunnvor Stallybrass), *The Wanderer*. London: Souvenir Press, 2012.

61 *We're the last ones here* . . . Colin Thubron, *In Siberia*. London: Chatto, 2008.

65 *He ordered them* . . . *The Historie and Cronicles of Scotland written and collected by Robert Lindesay of Pitscottie*. ed. A.J.G Mackay. Edinburgh: Wm Blackwood & Sons, 1899.

73 *The poverty of the place* . . . Charles Darwin, *The Voyage of the Beagle*. London: Simon & Schuster, 2014.

76 *Stands in the middle* . . . Darwin, *ibid.*

80 *The road lay* . . . Darwin, *ibid.*

80 *I take refuge in* . . . W.G. Sebald, *Vertigo*. London: Vintage, 2002.

80 *More and more* . . . Dunmore, *ibid.*

82 *You will find nothing there* . . . J.L. Borges in Bruce Chatwin, Paul Theroux, Jeff Gnass, *Nowhere Is a Place: Travels in Patagonia*. San Francisco: Sierra Club Books, 1985.

82 *In Patagonia the monotony* . . . W.H. Hudson, *Idle Days in Patagonia* London: Dent, 1923.

82 *The experience of Patagonia* . . . Brian Keenan and John McCarthy, *Between Extremes*. London: Black Swan, 1999.

84 *Over us the booming* . . . Dante Alighieri (trans. Henry Francis Cary), *Dante's Inferno*. Oxford: Oxford University Press, 1923.

88 *At intervals it* . . . Herman Melville, *Moby Dick*. London: Penguin, 1994.

91 *Most of us know* . . . C.S. Lewis, *The Voyage of the Dawn Treader*. London: Fontana Lions, 1980.

96 *Let them give glory* . . . Isaiah 42:12, King James Bible.

100 *Observing that* . . . Diana Souhami, *Selkirk's Island*. London: Weidenfeld and Nicolson, 2001.

105 *So here I am* . . . Anonymous (trans. Helen Bacovcin), *The Way of a Pilgrim*. New York: Doubleday, 2003.

106 *Born free, but* . . . Jean-Jacques Rousseau, *Of the Social Contract and Other Political Writings*. London: Penguin, 2012.

108 *I know men will* . . . Jean-Jacques Rousseau, *Reveries of the Solitary Walker*. Oxford: Oxford World Classics, 2011.

110 *No foreclosures of* . . . Herman Melville, *Typee: A Peep at Polynesian Life*. London: Wordsworth Classics, 1994.

112 *The idea of holiness* . . . Adam Nicolson, *Sea Room*. London: Harper-Collins, 2001.

114 *To approach these* . . . Robert Byron, *The Station – Travels to the Holy Mountain of Greece*. London: Duckworth, 1928.

118 *Whose name and history* . . . Nancy Campbell, *The Library of Ice*. London: Simon & Schuster, 2018.

120 *No man is an island* . . . John Donne, *Devotions upon Emergent Occasions*. New York: Cosimo, 2010.

120 *Nowhere can man* . . . Marcus Aurelius (trans. Maxwell Staniforth), *Meditations*. Harmondsworth: Penguin Classics, 1964.

124 *We are seized by* . . . Christiane Ritter (trans. Jane Degras), *A Woman in the Polar Night*. London: Allen & Unwin, 1954.

124 *Bethink thee* . . . Marcus Aurelius, *ibid*.

131 *There is a pleasure* . . . G.G. Byron, 'Childe Harold's Pilgrimage' in *The Collected Works of Lord Byron Vol II*. London: John Murray, 1821.

135 *A map of the world* . . . Oscar Wilde, 'The Soul of Man' in *The Complete Works of Oscar Wilde: Volume IV: Criticism*. Oxford: Oxford University Press, 2007.

137 *He journeyed further* . . . E.G.R. Taylor, 'A Letter Dated 1577 from Mercator to John Dee' in *Imago Mundi*, Vol. XIII. Routledge, 1956.

141 *By a kind of* . . . James Romm, *The Edges of the Earth in Ancient Thought*. Princeton: Princeton University Press, 1992.

141 *May I be an* . . . from K.H. Jackson, *A Celtic Miscellany*. Harmondsworth: Penguin, 1971.

152 *In Lydia, the islands* . . . Pliny, *Natural History*. Vol. II. London: H.G. Bohn, 1855.

152 *Credulous Pliny* . . . Annie Dillard, *Teaching a Stone to Talk*. Edinburgh: Canongate, 2016.

157 *There was nothing new* . . . Mitchell Symons, *Desert Island Discs: Flotsam & Jetsam*. London: Bantam, 2012.

161 *The daily log entries* . . . Keith Brockie, *One Man's Island*. London: Dent, 1984.

161 *a delightful residence* . . . W.J. Eggeling, *The Isle of May*. Edinburgh: Oliver & Boyd, 1960.

162 *September 1st, 1947* . . . Eggeling, *ibid*.

163 *Look, stranger on* . . . W.H. Auden, 'Seascape' in *Collected Poems*. New York: Vintage, 1991.

167 *Already self-sufficient* . . . A.J.W. Taylor and J.T. Shurley, 'Some Antarctic Troglodytes'. *International Review of Applied Psychology*, 29: 1971.

168 *He had a strong* . . . quoted in Diana Souhami, *ibid*.

170 *Sometimes I like* . . . William Morris quoted in Lavinia Greenlaw, *Questions of Travel: William Morris in Iceland*. London: Notting Hill, 2016.

170 *And now* . . . Daniel Defoe, *Robinson Crusoe*. Ware: Wordsworth Classics, 1999.

172 *Thick as autumn leaves* . . . R.L. Stevenson, *Treasure Island*. London: Cassell, 1883.

174 *Haply some philanthropic* . . . Robert Browning, *Aristophanes' Apology*. London: Smith, Elder & Co, 1875.

174 *Clothes and bedding* . . . Diana Souhami, *ibid*.

176 *Eleven or twelve renegades* . . . George Shelvocke, *A Voyage Round the World by Way of the Great South Sea*. London: Cassell, 1928.

181 *Rub and polish our brain* . . . Montaigne quoted in John Jeffries Martin, 'Montaigne in Italy' in John Jeffries Martin, ed., *The Renaissance World*. London: Routledge, 2015.

182 *If we can* . . . D.W. Winnicott, quoted in Adam Phillips, *Winnicott*. London: Penguin, 2007.

183 *Do I contradict* . . . Walt Whitman, 'Song of Myself' in Walt Whitman, *Leaves of Grass*. Boston: Thayer and Eldridge, 1860.

185 *My survey of Raasay* . . . James Boswell, *The Journal of a Tour to the Hebrides*. Oxford: Oxford University Press, 1948.

192 *I was born before* . . . Edwin Muir, *An Autobiography*. Edinburgh: Canongate, 1993.

198 *But the love of* . . . Sir Walter Scott, *The Pirate*. Edinburgh: Archibald Constable, 1822.

203 *Ah yes, nothing* . . . William Heinesen (trans. Tiina Nunnally), *Laterna Magica*. Washington: Fjord Press, 1987.

205 *But he was homeless and* . . . William Heinesen, *ibid*.

205 *Our Pinnace return'd* . . . quoted in Diana Souhami, *ibid*.

207 *He had so much* . . . Diana Souhami, *ibid*.

208 *Comes over one* . . . D.H. Lawrence, *Sea and Sardinia*. Cambridge: Cambridge University Press, 2002.

210 *Absolutely alone* . . . D.H. Lawrence, 'The Man Who Loved Islands' in *Selected Short Stories*. London: Penguin, 2007.

211 *We feel we're not* . . . D.H. Lawrence, *ibid*.

211 *I don't care for* . . . Geoff Dyer, *Out of Sheer Rage*. Edinburgh: Canongate, 1997.

212 *Of course I am happy* . . . Peter Matthiessen, *The Snow Leopard*. London: Chatto, 1979.

212 *Its excruciating purity* . . . Peter Matthiessen, *End of the Earth: Voyages to Antarctica*. Washington D.C.: National Geographic, 2003.

225 *The severity of this* . . . Marlo Willows, *Health Status in Lowland Medieval Scotland: A Regional Analysis of Four Skeletal Populations*. Doctoral thesis, submitted University of Edinburgh, 2016.

228 *It walks teetering* . . . Annie Dillard, *Teaching a Stone to Talk*. Edinburgh: Canongate, 2016.

230 *Never consorted at all* . . . Herman Melville, *Moby Dick*. London: Penguin, 1994.

MAPS & ILLUSTRATIONS

All maps marked NLS are courtesy of the National Library of Scotland.

35 Samoa by George Cram (1896). Chromograph.

38 Iona. *Blaeu Atlas Maior,* Volume 6, *Æbudæ Insulæ sive Hebrides* (1662–5) (NLS 108520521).

40 West Scotland. *Philips' Chamber of Commerce Atlas: A Graphic Survey of the World's Trade with a Commercial Compendium and Gazetteer Index* (George Philip & Son, London: The London Geographical Institute, Liverpool: Philip, Son & Nephew, 1914). Courtesy of University of Texas.

41 Great Britain. Directorate Of Colonial Surveys, and Great Britain. (1954) www.loc.gov/item/2009578551/.

44 Satellite view of Hawaii archipelago (USA). (Taken 27 May 2003) Image courtesy Jacques Descloitres, MODIS Land Rapid Response Team at NASA GSFC.

44 Hawaii. *Carte des Iles Sandwich* by Rigobert Bonne (1788).

46 Walden Pond. *Map of Concord Massachusetts 1852 made by Henry F. Walling showing names of landowners and district boundaries.* Courtesy of Harvard Map Collection.

48 Map of the wanderings of Odysseus, after Otho Cushing in Charles Lamb, *The Adventures of Ulysses* (Boston: Ginn & Company, 1894, 1917), frontispiece. Courtesy of Harvard's Centre for Hellenic Studies.

50 Blaeu Map of the Kingdom of Norway. *Norvegia Regnum* (1662).

57 Prison Islands: a) Château d'If by N. Tassin, published in Paris by Sébastien Cramoisy (1636); b) Alcatraz from Angel Island: the Ellis Island of the West by Mary Ellen Bamford (1917), courtesy of San Francisco Public Library; c) Ellis Island, from T. Bradford, *An Illustrated Atlas, Geographical, Statistical, and Historical, of the United States, and the Adjacent Countries* (1839).

59 Distributions of the Andaman tribes based on E.H. Man, from *On the Aboriginal Inhabitants of the Andaman Islands* (1885, reprinted 1932).

63 Inch Garvie. OS 25-inch, Linlithgowshire III.9 (Dalmeny; Dunfermline) (1896) (NLS 82895136).

64 Firth of Forth Land Utilisation Survey 1932–1933. Sheet 68 (NLS 74425099).

64 *The Bass Rock from the South* by John Abraham Slezer (circa 1700). Courtesy of National Library of Scotland.

66 Firth of Forth Land Utilisation Survey 1932–1933. Sheet 68 (NLS 74425099).

69 Barra. *The south part of Long Island from Bara Head to Benbecula I*, Plate XXVIII of Murdoch Mackenzie's *A maratim survey of Ireland and the west of Great Britain*, vol. II (1776) (NLS 74400896).

74 Chiloé (Chile) – in Enrique Espinoza, *Geografía Descriptiva de la República de Chile*. Map 33 by L. Fuentes, F.A. 1885. Courtesy of Biblioteca Nacional de Chile.

75 Chile, by Nicolas Sanson (1670). Courtesy of Biblioteca Nacional de Chile.

78 Pacific Ocean Communications. *Philips' Chamber of Commerce Atlas* (1914). Courtesy of University of Texas.

81 Tierra del Fuego. From James Weddell, *A voyage towards the South Pole, performed in the years 1822–24* (1827).

84 Falkland Islands. *Carte Des Îles Malouines ou Falkland* by Ètienne André Philippe de Prétot (1771).

87 South Georgia and Bird Island. G.W. Colton, *Colton's Atlas of the World Illustrating Physical and Political Geography*, Vol. 1 (New York, 1855).

89 South Orkney. From *The South Shetland and South Orkney Islands with the tracks of the several discoverers*, by the Hydrographic Office, 1839. Courtesy of the National Maritime Museum, Greenwich, London.

90 *Wave Clouds from the South Sandwich Islands* by Jeff Schmaltz. Courtesy of NASA.

95 Tollcross traffic islands. Edinburghshire III.11 (1933) (NLS 82877454).

98 North Ronaldsay. OS one-inch Scotland, popular edition, sheet 5 – Orkney Islands (North) (1931) (NLS 744000495.1).

100 Juan Fernandez. From *Atlas de la historia física y política de Chile* by Claudio Gay (1854). Courtesy of Biblioteca Nacional de Chile.

102 Athos. 3rd Military Mapping Survey of Austria-Hungary (1899).

105 Solovetsky Island. Русский: Большой Соловецкий остров CC Licence 4.0 Wikimedia Commons.

107 St Peter's Island. *L'ile de St. Pierre ou de J.J. Rousseau dans le lac de Bienne 1817* by Christoph Rheiner. Courtesy of Swiss National Library.

109 Athos. British War Office, Geographical Section, General Staff (1908). Courtesy of University of Bordeaux.

111 Marquesas Islands. Map of Marquesas Islands in Herman Melville, *Narrative of a Four Month's Residence among the Natives of a Valley of the Marquesas Islands; or, A Peep at Polynesian Life.* (London: John Murray, 1846).

115 Mount Athos peninsula. Piri Reis (Turkish, 1465–1555), 'Leaf from Book on Navigation'; seventeenth to eighteenth century, ink, paint and gold on paper. Courtesy of Walters Art Museum (W.658.49A).

119 Upernavik. *Carte du Groenland en langue danoise* (1937). Courtesy of Bibliothèque Nationale de France.

121 Mount Athos by Bartolommeo dalli Sonetti (circa 1485) from an *Isolario* (island book) of 58ff dedicated to Giovanni Mozenico, Doge of Venice 1475–85.

123 United States Central Intelligence Agency. *Norway. 6-62.* (1962). Retrieved from the Library of Congress, www.loc.gov/item/74693762/.

125 Edge Island. *Karte von Spitzbergen, einem arktischen Archipel, der zu Norwegen gehört* by Carl Schmidt (1914).

130 Map of the Faroe Islands. image extracted from p. 94 of *The Faröe Islands . . . With map and illustrations* by Joseph Russell Jeaffreson (1894). Courtesy of the British Library.

133 Greenland. *Carte du Groenland en langue danoise* (1937). Courtesy of Bibliothèque Nationale de France.

135 *Utopia* by Abraham Ortelius (1595). Courtesy of the King Baudouin Foundation.

136 Mercator's Arctic *Septentrionalium Terrarum descriptio* from G. Mercator and J. Hondius, *Atlas* (1606). Courtesy of Geographicus Rare Antique Maps.

137 Cape Verde/The Hesperides. *Insulae de Cabo Verde, Olim Hesperides, sive Gorgades* by Gerard Valck (1709–18).

146 Lake Titicaca, Peru, from H.C. Carey and I. Lea, *American Atlas* (Philadelphia, 1827). Courtesy of American Library of Congress.

148 United States Central Intelligence Agency. Peru. 5-70. Washington (1970). Retrieved from the Library of Congress, www.loc.gov/item/gm71001175/.

151 Taquile Island, Lake Titicaca. Map SD19-14 Puno, Peru; Bolivia. US
& National Imaging and Mapping Agency (1977). Courtesy of University
153 of Texas Library.

159 Isle of May. John Thomson, William Johnson, Fife with Kinross Shire. (1827) (NLS 744000166.1).

162 Isle of May. *Beschrijvinge van een deel vann Schottlandt van Bambourg tot Aberdein* by Lucas Janzsoon Waghenaer 1535–1606 (NLS 499.1).

169 Weddell Sea Area with inset of Brunt Ice Shelf by Paul Torode. Courtesy of Paul Torode (2012).

171 Brunt Ice Shelf and the Halloween Crack, by the European Space Agency (2017). Courtesy of the European Space Agency. Contains modified Copernicus Sentinel data (2017), processed by ESA.

173 Elephant Island. *The South Shetland and South Orkney Islands with the tracks of the several discoverers.* (1908). Courtesy of the Hydrographic Office.

175 Robben Island. *Carte de la Baye de la Table et Rade du Cap de Bonne Esperance* by Jacques Nicolas Bellin (1764). Courtesy of Geographicus Rare Antique Maps.

177 Sula Sgeir. OS six-inch series. Ross and Cromarty – Isle of Lewis Sheet I (includes: Barvas) (1898) (NLS: 76344041.1).

184 Skye. Map of the Clans of Scotland, from *Historical Geography of the Clans of Scotland* by Thomas Brumby Johnston and James A. Robertson. 1899.

187 Zamalek, River Nile. *Historische Karte von Kairo, Ägypten* by Alexander Nicohosoff (1933).

189 Pentland Firth. J. Bennett and R. Sayer, *A new chart of the north coast of Scotland with . . . the Orkney Islands* (1781) (NLS 744000304.1).

191 Orkney Islands by Murdoch Mackenzie (Senior) (1750) (NLS 85449271).

193 Rousay etc. OS sheet 5 – Orkney Islands (North) (1931) (NLS 744000495.1).

195 Stewart Island/Rakiura. *Carte de la côte méridionale de l'Ile de Tawaï-Poénammou (Nouvelle-Zélande)* by Jules Alphonse Rene Poret de Blosseville. From *Hydrographie-Atlas*, Paris, 1826, plate 45.

199 Hoy. Claes Janszoon Vooght, Johannes van Keulen. *Nieuwe paskaart van de Orcades Eylanden / door Vooght geometra* (1695) (NLS 514.1).

204 Orkney Islands by Murdoch Mackenzie (Senior) (1750) (NLS 85449271.1).

206 Juan Fernandez. Jacques Nicolas Bellin, *Carte particulière de l'Isle de Juan Fernandés'* (1753).

209 Sardinia. *Antiche mappa della Sardegna* by Sigismondo Asquer (sixteenth century).

211 Îles d'Hyères. Cassini, César-François, et al. *Carte de France* (1756). Retrieved from the Library of Congress, www.loc.gov/item/gm72002942/.

213 Gold Coast, North Atlantic by Antonio Sanches (1633). Courtesy of Royal Museums Greenwich.

216 A faithful reproduction of *Carta marina* (a wall map of Scandinavia by Olaus Magnus published in 1539, this copy 1572). Courtesy of Royal Library, National Library of Sweden.

219 Firth of Forth. *Carte du Golphe d'Edinburgh* by J.N. Bellin (1757) (NLS 74401116.1).

221 Edinburgh. OS Edinburghshire III.11 (1933) (NLS 82877454.1).

224 Isle of May outer. John Ainslie, southeast section: *A chart of part of the South of Scotland, from Berwick upon Tweed to Skateraw Harbour in the County of Kincardine . . .* (1785) (NLS 74401115.1).

227 Galapagos Islands. *Chart of the Galapagos: Surveyed in the Merchant-Ship* Rattler *and Drawn by Captain James Colnett of the Royal Navy in 1793* (1794), engraved by T. Foot. Courtesy of the World Digital Library.

229 The Solar System, from *Astronomical Diagrams* by James Reynolds and John Emslie (1860). Courtesy of the National Maritime Museum, Greenwich, London.

GAVIN FRANCIS is an award-winning writer and GP. He is the author of four books of non-fiction, including *Adventures in Human Being*, which was a *Sunday Times* bestseller and won the Saltire Scottish Non-Fiction Book of the Year Award, and *Empire Antarctica*, which won Scottish Book of the Year in the SMIT Awards and was shortlisted for both the Ondaatje and Costa Prizes. He has written for the *Guardian*, *The Times*, the *New York Review of Books* and the *London Review of Books*. His work is published in eighteen languages. He lives in Edinburgh, Scotland.

@gavinfranc | gavinfrancis.com

CANON‖GATE

Cover design by Gill Heeley
Cover image: Map of Treasure Island. Robert Louis Stevenson,
Treasure Island (1883) Cassell